Chris—

you represent
one of the great
blessings of our
time at Eastern.

With great affection
and appreciation
Bob Sleigh

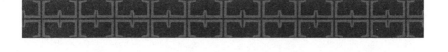

AMBASSADORS *of*

H O P E

HOW CHRISTIANS CAN RESPOND TO THE WORLD'S TOUGHEST PROBLEMS

ROBERT A. SEIPLE

InterVarsity Press
Downers Grove, Illinois

9|15|08

InterVarsity Press
P.O. Box 1400, Downers Grove, IL 60515-1426
World Wide Web: www.ivpress.com
E-mail: mail@ivpress.com

InterVarsity Press® is the book-publishing division of InterVarsity Christian Fellowship/USA®, a student movement active on campus at hundreds of universities, colleges and schools of nursing in the United States of America, and a member movement of the International Fellowship of Evangelical Students. For information about local and regional activities, write Public Relations Dept., InterVarsity Christian Fellowship/USA, 6400 Schroeder Rd., P.O. Box 7895, Madison, WI 53707-7895, or visit the IVCF website at <www.ivcf.org>.

Cover design: Cindy Kiple

Cover images: Anthony Marsland/Getty Images

ISBN 0-8308-3223-8

Printed in Canada ∞

Library of Congress Cataloging-in-Publication Data

Seiple, Robert A., 1942-
  Ambassadors of hope: how Christians can respond to the world's
  toughest problems / Robert A. Seiple.
     p. cm.
  Includes bibliographical references.
  ISBN 0-8308-3223-8 (alk. paper)
  1. Christianity and international affairs. 2. Church charities. 3.
  Non-governmental organizations. I. Title.
  BR115.17S42 2004
  261.8'7—dc22
                                                        2004009779

P	16	15	14	13	12	11	10	9	8	7	6	5	4	3	2	1
Y	17	16	15	14	13	12	11	10	09	08	07	06	05	04		

Dedicated, with pleasure, to

The 2000 Cohort

Templeton Honors Program,

Eastern University.

Emerging leaders, every one of them.

CONTENTS

ACKNOWLEDGMENTS

I am grateful to God for providing me a lifetime of experience on both the balconies and the dance floors of the world. World Vision, particularly, opened my eyes and broke my heart. My eleven years at the helm of World Vision, Inc. has been the highlight of my life, providing a vast reservoir of faces that continue to sweeten precious memories.

In making sense of what I witnessed, the scholarly reflections of friends like John Paul Lederach and Miroslav Volf were indispensable. I lift them up and call them blessed!

Much better writers than I were enlisted in the editing process. Chris Hall, professor of biblical and theological studies at Eastern University; Tim Dean, formerly the senior editor of the BBC's World News Service and now executive secretary of the First Step Forum; Dennis Hoover, vice president for research and publication at the Institute for Global Engagement—all in turn took the manuscript one positive step further. Al Hsu, associate editor at InterVarsity Press, led a team of editors that demonstrated insight and patience as multiple drafts were carefully screened.

And Anne Cohen, executive assistant at IGE, ensured that each draft was carefully transcribed, maintaining the process and holding the logistical threads together.

Finally, my wife and best friend, Margaret Ann—a travel partner to most of the world—more than anyone else made sure that my Type A personality did not trample on the dignity and sanctity of those we felt called to serve. I have been blessed and honored by this "ambassador of hope."

1

RELEVANCE

Getting There with Something to Say

I am only one; but still I am one. I cannot do everything, but still I can do something. I will not refuse to do something I can do.

HELEN KELLER

In the spring of 1988, I was returning to Vietnam for the first time in two decades. I had last been in the country for a thirteen-month tour of duty starting in 1967, courtesy of the United States Marine Corps. I returned now not as a Marine but as president of World Vision. The objective of the trip was to reopen Vietnam for World Vision's humanitarian aid work, which had been severely curtailed since 1975, the year Saigon fell.

For me, the trip stoked the smoldering emotions that anyone who served during the war inevitably carries with them for a lifetime. Expectations and hopes for a better future mixed painfully with memories of fear, frustration, separation from loved ones and the loss of close friends. Yet I could not wait to get there, and I brought both my wife, Margaret Ann, and our youngest son, twelve-year-old Jesse, with me.

World Vision is the largest privately funded relief and development agency in the world. Today it works in more than one hundred countries, primarily with the poorest of the poor and those most vulnerable, namely children. Health care, microenterprise and development are just some of the specific ways World Vision works to remove stumbling blocks for children. All of this work had been taking place in South Vietnam before 1975, and the possibility of reentering Vietnam after all those years was exciting, to say the least. We were also anxious, because we were not certain how Vietnamese officials would receive us. In fact, we felt obliged to carry a little extra "firepower" of our own: a letter affirming our visit from President Ronald Reagan, who was unarguably the most powerful leader in the world in 1988.

In many ways, the trip was a disaster. We were there on a humanitarian mission, seeking to restart a comprehensive ministry in a country that was needier at that time than it was before 1975. The government officials with whom we interacted, however, only wanted to talk about the war: they had won; we had lost. This was the message drummed into our collective heads at every stop along the way. The tone of conversations was relentlessly hostile; the substance was ideological. And the upshot was clear: could a "Western" nongovernmental organization (NGO) be of any help to Vietnam?

And the presidential letter was like a red flag waved in front of a raging bull. These officials were not about to accept a letter from Reagan— the man who had most clearly articulated the "evil" of communism—as the third-party endorsement we had assumed would be necessary for World Vision to reenter the country.

Each day brought more of the same—more meetings with hostile officials, more anger vented against America, more savoring of the irony: an American humanitarian effort to help those who had "won the war." By the last day of our trip, our hopes were sagging. We were enduring one final meeting, seated across yet another table, listening to yet another tirade launched against our mission. Our bags were packed and we were ready to go. We were about to limp out of Hanoi.

As the meeting was drawing to a close, the communist official across the table was somehow inspired to ask one more question: "Does anyone have anything else they would like to say?" There was a momentary silence, then a young voice at the end of the table said, "Yes, I do." It was Jesse. Margaret Ann and I looked at one another, and I am sure we were thinking the same thing: "What else can go wrong?" Our communist hosts seemed to be interested, if not amused, by the participation of this young man. All eyes turned to Jesse. He now had the floor, and it was immediately clear that he was not going to relinquish it until he said what he had to say.

"I think you ought to listen to my dad," he began. "I know my dad. He only wants to help you. He will help you if you let him." That was it. Nothing more. The meeting was over. Everyone from the communist delegation got up and rushed over to shake Jesse's hand. They wanted to have their pictures taken with him. I looked at Margaret Ann with one of those "who could have imagined" looks, then quietly folded my Ronald Reagan letter and stuck it back into my pocket.

The meeting was over but the door was opened. World Vision was allowed to come back into Vietnam; indeed we were encouraged to do so. Today that organization is the largest NGO in the country, working from north to south with a great deal of credibility due to the countless people who are being helped. And all because a twelve-year-old had the courage to speak truth to power.

THE TIME TO SPEAK

Many of us fantasize from time to time about "speaking truth to power." You may not think you will be in a position to confront government officials, yet none of us have any inkling of how our own lives might unfold. Take me, for example. I started my professional life in higher education, and when the call came from World Vision I was happily involved as president of Eastern College and Eastern Baptist Theological Seminary. World Vision became an eleven-year blessing for me, introducing me to a world of complexity, danger, hurts and massive vulnerability. I was shot at in Sarajevo and in the Gaza Strip. I experienced many a meal in mud huts throughout Africa. I walked past the bleaching bones of genocide victims in places like Rwanda and Cambodia.

Then, in 1998, President Clinton asked me to come to Washington and be the first Ambassador-at-Large for International Religious Freedom. The faces of the poor gave way to the faces of the powerful. I traveled under the flag of the greatest superpower in the history of the world. For the first time, I also heard the cries of the persecuted church and saw the faces of those who were desperate for an advocate to help ease the pain.

I planned none of this, but these experiences now compel me to speak out for what I see in the world and to speak up for those who have no voice.

Too often truth has been trivialized while secular power has been puffed up. Both concepts need to be rehabilitated, and those who would attempt such a task are legion. Unfortunately, as we look at any aspect of our world, it seems that power is dominating the struggle. The need for creative and truth-loving engagement in global affairs is urgent, and the opportunities are more abundant than most people realize. Always remember this: you have just as great a possibility of being called on to speak truth to power as I have, or as my twelve-year-old son has.

Jesus tells us, "I am the . . . truth" (John 14:6). We who are Christians believe that our faith offers solutions to some of the intractable conflicts in the world. Why, then, do we seem to have so much difficulty articulating this truth, bearing witness to the hope that lies within us (see 1 Peter 3:15)? Why do we appear to be so passionate about the world that "God so loved" and yet make such anemic efforts in engaging that world? Why does the greatest message ever delivered to humanity reside in so many people with so little tangible relevance and so little impact on the rest of the world in which we live?

This book is about a lot of things: leadership, sustainable solutions, effective global engagement and reconciliation. But more than any one of these, this book is written for those who want their faith to count, for those who want to make a legitimate difference, to have a credible impact in the world in which they have chosen to engage. This book is for those who want their faith to work in the difficult corners of the world, those cruel edges where evil seems to dominate and the battle "against the rulers, against the authorities, against the powers of this dark world" appears to be most intense (Ephesians 6:12).

At times, *Ambassadors of Hope* will read like a personal memoir. I do not apologize for that. As Jeremiah said so eloquently, "His word is in my heart like a fire, a fire shut up in my bones. I am weary of holding it in; indeed, I cannot" (Jeremiah 20:9-10). I have been allowed to see the world at its worst, to view evil up close and to experience a grace that was always in much greater supply than the destructive wickedness so prevalent around me. I have come to realize that it is not enough for my faith to work in the comfortable confines of my church, my community and this powerful nation that has shielded my life from so much potential harm. My faith has to work in the hard places. My theology has to touch the ground where people are hurting.

A faith that is shielded from the world's realities ultimately will lose its power. This book arises from my hope and conviction that by sharing some of my experiences over the past three decades, today's emerging leaders—those trying to make sense of the world in which they live, those looking for a theological worldview relevant for such a time as this—might be encouraged in their engagement of an ever more complex globe. If I can help someone else experience the sure-footed relevancy of a faith that can hold up under the most difficult circumstances imaginable, this book will have been worth writing.

In our generation we have seen war, genocide, ethnic cleansing and mass killings of innocent civilians; the list of atrocities appears to be end-less. Somalia, Rwanda, Bosnia, Kosovo, Sierra Leone, Indonesia—all suggest that evil is alive and well. But where in such a world does the Christian faith make a difference? How do we ensure that our witness is credible? Will that witness ultimately have an impact, that is, will our Christian faith be relevant in the world today?

We want to represent the truth. Yet we live in a world where there is ample testimony to the fact that power has run amok. Opportunities for speaking truth to power are available, but sometimes we fail to speak, or we intervene too late or in an inappropriate way. Let me explain through two examples, one from the Old Testament and one from ten years ago.

INDIVIDUAL AND CORPORATE FAILINGS

The little-known biblical figure Ahimaaz was the son of Zadok, a high priest (see 2 Samuel 18:19-31). At the very least he was a young preacher's kid, historically always a difficult cross to bear.

Ahimaaz enters our biblical text during a terrible civil war between King David and his rebel son, Absalom. The last great battle of the war has been fought. Absalom has managed to get himself tangled in a tree. Joab, David's military surrogate, comes upon Absalom in that state and kills him. The victory of the day is sealed, and it is now time to take the good news of the victory back to the king.

The prospect of taking such news to a powerful king is very appeal-ing to Ahimaaz. He wants to be the bearer of glad tidings, but Joab ar-gues with him. It is not immediately obvious why Joab reacted this way. Yet he was certainly aware that bringing this truth to power—the rebel Absalom is dead and victory is won—had to be carried out with great care.

A Cushite is assigned the task, yet no sooner does the Cushite set out to deliver the news than Ahimaaz begins his pleading once more:

"Please, please, can I go too?" Again Joab tries to impress on Ahimaaz that there is no personal gain in this venture. Finally, however, as if to put a stop to the persistent and youthful pleadings, Joab relents, probably hoping there has been enough time for the Cushite to get to the king and make Ahimaaz nothing more than a moot point.

But Ahimaaz is also clever. He knows a shortcut and ultimately overtakes the Cushite and gets into the king's presence first. He is bringing truth to power, taking the good news of victory to David. It is immediately obvious, however, that David is interested in Absalom's safety. When he inquires concerning this, Ahimaaz can only sputter lamely, "I saw great confusion . . . but I don't know . . ." It is at this point that David says, "Stand aside and wait here."

A critical time, a critical conversation, an important dialogue with a key power broker of the day—and Ahimaaz was asked to step aside. He was willing. He was persistent. He was motivated. He was physically able. But when he found himself in the presence of the king, the mover and shaker of Judaic antiquity, he was asked to step aside because he had nothing to say. Ultimately then, this became a wasted opportunity, one brief, shining moment destroyed, one great hour of sharing lost. Ahimaaz was relegated to obscurity. He got there with nothing to say.

Fast forward to April 1994 in the small African country of Rwanda. Like so many countries in Africa, Rwanda was emerging from a period of painful colonization. Even with a common language and for the most part a common faith (Christianity), the Rwandans shared a history pockmarked with tribal warfare. Two distinct groups of people emerged from one tribe: a majority Hutu, who were predominantly farmers, and a Tutsi minority, who were better educated and now held many of the key governing positions in Rwanda.

Over the decades, many of the distinctions blurred between these two factions, but there still remained a great deal of animosity that could burst forth at any moment. On April 6, 1994, a plane carrying the president of Rwanda was shot down while attempting to land in Kigali, the capital. To this day, the perpetrators have not been identified, but the assassination carried more than enough impetus to provoke and launch a systematic genocide of the Tutsis by the Hutus. In the next few months, somewhere between 800,000 and 1,000,000 Tutsis would be massacred. It was the most efficient killing of a people—machetes, clubs and spears notwithstanding—since Hiroshima and Nagasaki.

The unfolding events were broadcast to the entire world, and the visual effects of the genocide were traumatizing to all. Miles of refugees, walking with a vacant look of unspeakable horror etched on their faces, provided images that are just as vivid today as they were then. Heaps of bodies, stacked like cordwood along the roads. Villages burning. The survivors, more dead than alive, carrying the stench of murdered families as they aimlessly moved through the Rwandan countryside. These were the pictures that shocked the world and determined the foreign policy of many countries that would eventually become involved.

There was failure on many fronts. The international community was reluctant to step in. The last remaining superpower, the United States, had just painfully extricated itself from a problem it had sought to fix in Somalia. International organizations, most notably the United Nations, were totally inept.

Seeking to establish their bona fides as actively involved relief organizations, NGOs followed the scent of the international media to the refugee camps on the borders, now populated by Hutus in full flight. (The Rwandan Patriotic Front, comprising Tutsis from neighboring Uganda, was able to get the upper hand militarily, and the Hutus, fearing retaliation, left the country by the millions.) In what became one of the most devastating black marks in the history of NGO involvement in the world, these private organizations became the food chain into the camps, prompting one writer to refer to them disdainfully as the "caterers of génocidaires."[1]

The world would be further shocked to know that the Rwandan church in some cases actively participated in the genocide. Priests would be called to task. Nuns would stand trial in the International Criminal Tribunal. To be sure, there were exceptions—and exceptional acts of valor. But unfortunately the heroes of the church are, for the most part, dead. The sting of a failed faith lingers to this day. When this tender subject is broached inside Rwanda, the question one often hears is this: "And where was the church outside Rwanda?"

The response—and lack of it—to Rwanda's crisis represents a massive failure toward a people who were experiencing the ultimate indignity: the desecration of human life on a massive scale. The forces of reluctance, timidity and disinterest conspired together while people died by the hundreds of thousands.

Ahimaaz's failure was individual. The failure in Rwanda was corporate. Credibility was diminished, relevance was destroyed, and truth was lost on power. The indictment of the world concerning Rwanda was simply this: we were so late that our words were meaningless. In effect, we arrived with nothing to say.

NOTHING IS TOO DIFFICULT FOR THE LORD

We now live in the post-Cold War era. What we have painfully come to understand is that such a world can be more complex, more difficult and more dangerous than anything we have known to date. It is nothing short of frightening to realize that a genocide on the scale of the Rwandan massacre could have taken place within the last decade. Moreover, since Rwanda we also have had our sensibilities seared by Bosnia, Kosovo, Sierra Leone and Indonesia. We are not sure where this terrible litany will end.

What we do know is that people of faith and faith-based institutions are increasingly being invited to the secular table to bring their unique assets and perspectives to bear on solving such conflicts. Imagine, for example, the attractiveness of a sovereign God—"nothing is too difficult for the Lord"—in the face of conflicts that the secular world has deemed intractable. Imagine the appeal of reconciliation, the absolute heart of the Christian message, to a world that is looking for a solution that endures. Imagine hope made tangible by an empty tomb and by a church that has prevailed over the "gates of hell"—a tangibility held in the present that legitimates hope for the future.

The Christian has examples, models, principles, a sacred text and the One who has shown us in the most profound way that this is a world "God so loved." How then do we engage this world? How do we forge sustainable solutions? How do we engender legitimate hope for all those who have known nothing but dark despair? In short, how do we effectively and in a timely way "get there with something to say"? This book is written to address these questions. It is my hope that this exercise of global engagement will rejuvenate our faith, quicken our desire to be involved and make us more serious students of and sophisticated players in our Father's world.

These expectations are high; this book attempts a lot. But remember, once a twelve-year-old boy ventured to speak, and in so doing penetrated the communist hierarchy of Vietnam.

WHAT WE'RE FACING

2

CHALLENGE

Intractable Conflicts or Extraordinary Opportunities?

Past the seeker as he prayed came the crippled and the beggar and the
beaten. And seeing them . . . he cried, "Great God, how is it that a loving
creator can see such things and yet do nothing about them?" . . . God said,
"I did do something. I made you."

SUFI TEACHING

On the fifth of January 1991, an international event had profound
significance for the new post-Cold War era. In Mogadishu, Somalia, two
giant American helicopters took off, carrying the combined diplomatic
staffs of the United States and the Soviet Union. These were two countries
that had fought proxy wars in virtually every corner of the world. The
ideological struggle had been intense for more than forty years, and now
one of the theaters of this drama was being vacated by the main actors.

The irony was intense: two longtime antagonists on an American military aircraft, together leaving a land they had contested. The flow of
arms provided by both sides would cease, and the extension of superpower conflict would end. But Somalia was not receding into insignifi-
cance. Instead it was about to provide a case study and metaphor for the
most important new realities of our world.

News of the Americans and Soviets quitting Somalia was lost in the
midst of the Gulf War, which was beginning to capture the attention of

the media. But in this far-off corner of the world, a new sign of hope was made tangible. Perhaps a new world order was possible. Perhaps new rules could be written to govern this nascent geopolitical dynamic. Perhaps a peace dividend could be realized. It was a hopeful day and an extraordinary sight.

It could be forgiven if there was caution and perhaps even some cynicism lingering that day. There is a saying in Africa: "When two elephants fight, the ground gets trampled." It is also true that when two elephants make love, the ground is equally trampled. The change in Somalia brought many questions into relief. Would new rules emerge? Could Cold War manipulation and proxy warfare give way to a legitimate embrace of former enemies? Would partnerships emerge that would use our collective best instincts and highest values to create a different context? Would the end of a bipolar power struggle provide opportunities for a unified strategy toward the real problems in that world, or would distraction and disinterest conspire to produce a new series of conflicts even more complicated than the last?

Much has transpired in the past decade to give us a fairly objective answer to these questions. Today there are two all-consuming challenges that characterize the world in which we live: intractability (of long-running conflicts that seem to defy solution) and diversity (and the attendant inability to live with our deepest differences). These are the issues we will explore at great depth in the next two chapters. I will lay out the facts that have been demonstrated by world events: the issues and the statistics that have emerged from the conflicts of the past decade.

As one of my colleagues once said, "The difference between an optimist and a pessimist is that the pessimist has more facts!" Obviously much has gone wrong during this period. But before we get to the statistics and the issues, I want to present the assumptions, the definitions and the standard I am using for analyzing the role of Christians in global affairs and for evaluating whether or not our presence contributes toward enduring solutions.

A Helpful Metaphor

There is a wonderful visual metaphor for global engagement, which is also sometimes used to illustrate leadership: a split-screen picture of a dance floor and a balcony. Those on the balcony can observe and comment on what is going on below, but they are not involved. Those on the dance floor are very much involved; an exercise is being conducted that involves emotion, effort and engagement (all of which are sometimes messy: toes are stepped on, drinks are spilled, neckties are lost and so on). Of course, there are times in our lives when we may find ourselves on the balcony and there are times when we will be fully engaged on the dance floor. The question doesn't change, however, and it is simply this: From what perspective do *you* want to engage your world? Do you want to be where the potential messiness is? Or does the balcony provide a safe haven, a protected perspective, a good view from which to reflect on someone else's problems?

For Americans, it is sometimes extremely hard to be on that dance floor. We're part of a large, affluent and powerful country. It is easy for us to insulate ourselves from the difficult corners of the world. We live, so to speak, with a remote control in our hand. At any moment we can stop those terrible "pictures" from penetrating our minds and our consciousness. We live on the largest balcony in the world, and one has to make a conscious choice to leave that balcony and get "down and dirty" on the dance floor. The choice is ours, and therein lies the tension.

Some years ago I was traveling in Mozambique (just to the northeast of South Africa) during the long civil war between the forces of FRELIMO and those of RENAMO. FRELIMO represented the socialist government in power; RENAMO was the rebel group, sometimes called "freedom fighters" because they were ostensibly anticommunist. We flew to the northern part of the country, where World Vision was doing some work. We stayed in Quelimane, a town on the coast that was safe—hot showers, good food (giant prawns with Cajun sauce!), air-conditioning and sheets on the beds.

Every day we would fly out to the little village of Deere. It was not big enough to be called a town and it was not much as a village. Deere was essentially a place where people who had been wounded in the conflict, most of them innocent civilians, would come for medical attention in a World Vision clinic. Most of the victims were still severely traumatized and in a great deal of pain. When RENAMO rebels attacked villages, they intentionally traumatized the population by cutting off parts of the survivors' bodies. Throughout the clinic I saw people who had their noses, ears or even their eyelids cut off.

World Vision had a male nurse in Deere named Geraldo whose role was to take care of these people and to try to restore a measure of wholeness to them through his medical profession. We would fly to Deere in the morning, and Geraldo would make sure we saw life as he saw it. In a sense, he made sure we had a complete tour. It did not take long to realize that this was one of God's great human beings, with a heart for the ministry and a passion for people. He was absolutely the right person to be there. At four o'clock in the afternoon, it was time for us to be whisked out of town and back to Quelimane. We got to return to the balcony. As night fell, Geraldo continued life on the dance floor.

Two weeks after our visit, RENAMO attacked the village, knowing that there were people at Deere who were trying to help restore others to health. These people with demented minds bred out of a terrible civil conflict simply could not stomach the thought that there would be a person who would try to help their victims. They began to beat the people at the clinic. They destroyed the hospital and took Geraldo outside town. There they tied him to a tree and beat him to death.

Hearing the news left me weak and unnerved, and provided yet another sobering reality check concerning the world in which we live. As we look to engage what has become a very complicated, difficult and dangerous world, we must ask ourselves the question everyone has to answer: "Do I want to be up on the balcony, or do I want to be down on the dance floor?"

I spent eleven years as president of one of the world's largest private humanitarian aid agencies. For the past decade, coming home from a day's work has meant carrying with me the weight of the latest genocide, of the malnourishment of poverty, of the spiritual deformities that result from indulgent self-interest. I have been an eyewitness to so much of this chaos and human pain that I feel compelled to leave testimony to what I have seen, not as an apocalyptic pessimist or optimist looking for followers or dollars, but as a realist.

EFFECTIVE GLOBAL ENGAGEMENT

There are two concepts that I will use repeatedly in this book, and a short explanation might be helpful. Effective global engagement is both *credible* and *relevant*. Credibility is nothing more (and nothing less) than doing what we say we are going to do. If our global engagement is through the exercise of planting trees or drilling for pure water or vaccinating children, our credibility will be determined by performing those acts.

Relevancy takes us a step further. It speaks of impact. To use the same illustration, if we are planting trees, we need to plant and nourish them in a way that enables them to take firm root. If we are looking for water, we need to find it. If we are vaccinating children against deadly diseases, they'd better live. If these things do not happen, we have absolutely nothing to say, no witness to bring, no testimony that is relevant to the world that we have chosen to engage. It should be the passion and the absolute nonnegotiable bottom line that we will be both true to our task (we will do what we say we are going to do; thus we will be *credible*) and we will excel at what we do (there will be positive results that will impact a community, making our witness *relevant*).

THE SUSTAINABLE SOLUTION: RECONCILIATION

The ultimate sustainable solution to so many of the world's problems is *reconciliation*. That word has been around for more than two thousand years, and the need has been everywhere evident since Adam and Eve opted for the apple. Sometimes it is used improperly as an alternative word for *mediation* and *conflict resolution*. But each of these words has a different meaning. Let me illustrate this through an incident that took place in our Lord's life when he was confronted by a woman taken in adultery.

A group of lawyers and Pharisees bring a woman caught in the act of adultery to stand before Jesus. He is asked to mediate an issue, namely whether the law of Moses, which commanded stoning in such cases, was to be implemented. The mediation is between a Roman perspective that did not allow for the Jews to carry out death sentences and the Mosaic law. Jesus' mediation skills are superb: essentially he does nothing! He merely doodles in the sand and allows enough time to elapse for the tension and the emotions to begin to subside. Jesus employs a great deal of common sense here. It is very difficult, often impossible, for either side of a dispute to buy into the logic of resolution when emotions are operating at a fever pitch.

When Jesus finally speaks he gives us that great sentence: "If any one of you is without sin, let him be the first to throw a stone at her" (John 8:7). This is followed by more doodling in the sand, while his words begin to sink in and convict the crowd—from the oldest to the youngest, interestingly. Each individual personalizes the implications of Christ's statement, drops his stones, and the mob slowly begins to melt away. This is conflict resolution. The conflict was resolved, which is to say the accusers laid down their weapons when they came face to face with penetrating logic.

When successful, conflict resolution removes the threat of violence. It is a necessary precursor to something deeper: reconciliation. There is absolutely no chance for reconciliation while people are still throwing stones at one another. Until warring parties are separated, the components for true reconciliation will never have a chance.

True reconciliation is about changed hearts, something Jesus expects and empowers. In his intervention on behalf of the adulterous woman, Jesus assures her that there is no condemnation for what she has done. He does not condone her sin, but suggests to her, from the authority as her newfound Savior, that she leave her life of sin behind. This exercise involves a heart change for the woman. A permanent and positive change of heart is what reconciliation is all about.

Perhaps mediation can be done as a cognitive exercise, while conflict resolution is usually a logistical one—parting the antagonists, getting them to put their weapons aside. Reconciliation, by contrast, is a heart change, and for this reason it is the most difficult of the three to effect.

The shared helicopter ride high above Mogadishu symbolized a limited success in conflict resolution. It set the stage for other resolutions in the future, when meaningful mediation would have a better chance. But it was not reconciliation. Only a change of heart will bring reconciliation in the destructive conflicts and the regions of unrest that are so complex we think them to be intractable.

Reconciliation is the heart of the Christian gospel. It should also be the integrating and compelling vision we pursue in the twenty-first century. It is what Christians have to offer as we take a rightful seat at the table of global engagement. It is the sustainable solution for anyone who wants to turn credibility into relevance, for anyone whose desire it is to be effective on the dance floor and to glorify God in the process.

Reconciliation continues to be God's gift to us through his Son. The apostle Paul makes it clear that the baton has been passed and we too must now become agents of reconciliation:

> God was reconciling the world to himself in Christ, not counting men's sins against them. And he has committed to us the message of reconciliation. We are therefore Christ's ambassadors, as though God were making his appeal through us. We implore you on Christ's behalf: Be reconciled to God. (2 Corinthians 5:18-20)

Or course, I have merely scratched the surface; much remains to be unpacked in the pages of this book. With these metaphors, definitions and visions in mind, I want to return to the nature of the world that we see today, the size of the challenge, and why, for some, the conflicts continue to defy the promise of the end of the Cold War.

THE NATURE OF THE WORLD TODAY

Why does this world present such a daunting challenge for those of us who want to be actively engaged in it? Let me give you a statistical summary first. We have just finished the bloodiest century in the history of humanity. More than 100 million people were killed in war during the twentieth century alone. We have seen exponential growth in complex humanitarian emergencies that affect entire countries or entire people groups, from an average of five per year in 1980 to more than twenty-five per year today. There are now more than 10 million refugees in the world—5.8 million internally displaced and another 4.2 million pushed outside their nations' borders.[1] We used to lament the fact that there were 10 million AIDS orphans in Africa. That number today is 11 million in sub-Saharan Africa alone,[2] and only God knows what it will be ten years from now. Furthermore, there are still 32,000 children under the age of five who die every day from diseases long eradicated in the West.

Today more than 600 million people around the world are being persecuted for their faith—a staggering figure. The definition of that persecution includes beatings, rapes, killings and prolonged detentions without cause, all for exercising a universal right to believe and to worship as one sees fit.

These statistics are overwhelming. They can be paralyzing. As we contemplate the enormous amount of hurt that continues to exist in the twenty-first century, we might feel the world's problems are intractable.

"These are mere statistics," Joseph Stalin said, referring to the deaths of 15 million people in World War II. He ironically went on to say, "The death of an individual is a human tragedy." Specifically, then, what may make us think that the challenge is greater at this time than at any other time in history? What is new today that might suggest that a higher level of sophistication is necessary for those who feel called to global engagement? Let me suggest a number of relatively new and complicating factors that have sobered our enthusiasm from those heady days at the end of the Cold War.

First is the presence of *enduring despots*. It is amazing how many two-bit despots have had longevity in our post-Cold War environment. This phenomenon is not without irony, as politicians of stable countries come and go quickly, while a person like Slobodan Milosevic gets to lead his country through four wars in a decade. In the first Gulf War, Saddam Hussein lost big but claimed victory simply because he remained standing in the ring when the fight was over. The superpower constraints of the Cold War have been lifted, and sometimes this has accrued to the benefit of those who would be king.

Second is the proliferation of *identity conflicts*. Many of today's horrific civil conflicts fall along the lines of primary identity, such as ethnicity or religion, or both. We now take note of the height of one's cheekbones, how often one is called to prayer, what alphabet is used—all good examples of what Freud called "the narcissism of small differences." Diversity is good, except when it takes place in a hostile environment. Perhaps the single most important lesson of the last fifteen years is that no one wants to be a minority in a hostile environment. The mantra of survival is "Do it to them before they do it to you."

Third are the *refugees*. Refugees are no longer the unfortunate byproduct of a war: in many cases they are the goal. This is the other side of ethnic cleansing, that terrible trauma visited upon innocent civilians.

Fourth is the phenomenon of *intranational conflict*. Today's battles are within countries, even within neighborhoods, not between countries. We are seeing a new form of tribalism that is more horrific and destructive then we have ever seen before. Many of the conflicts are low-tech, producing high carnage. Note the point-blank bombardments that went on for years in Bosnia, and the clubs and machetes used in Rwanda with such devastating effectiveness. Conflicts like these tended to be genocidal in nature, and they all happened in a century when we said, "Never again."

Fifth, consider important new trends in *military doctrines*. For the past several years, the military has been the safest place to be. Almost 80 percent of all casualties in present-day conflicts are civilians, predominantly women and children. Protection of armed forces has been and continues to be a huge issue. The war in Kosovo makes the point. Although it was fought on the basis of a moral imperative, that moral imperative could not fly below fifteen thousand feet! We made a "foreign policy" decision that no amount of carnage on the ground was worth a single American life.

Sixth is the impact of *video technology,* commonly called the CNN Effect. Today it is all about "pictures." For Rwanda, it was the pictures that drove foreign policy. The United States had already established a series of decision points that had to be achieved before we would enter that country. We wanted clarity on security issues. We needed a precise definition of our role. We wanted clarity concerning an exit strategy, and so on. But once the American people saw those horrifying pictures of vulnerable humanity, their response to the carnage dictated our foreign policy. No more can we allow the fire to burn out on the back forty, so to speak. CNN is there to show us every graphic detail. Unfortunately one man's pictures are another man's death certificate. By the time we see the pictures, life has expired. Make no mistake about it; there is nothing preemptive or preventive in a foreign policy based on terrible pictures.

Finally, *Christians* have been part of the problem. That's right—for every good missionary story there is at least one bad one. Christians tend toward two extremes. The first is an emphasis on a privatized faith, a faith that obscures or dismisses the world and removes or isolates legitimate "neighbors." People look for God's will for their lives by asking, "What's in it for me?" Faith seems to be reduced to a personal self-help course, a way to get personal needs met.

At the other extreme we have a "ready, fire, aim" approach to problems overseas. Often we show little or no sensitivity to the state of faith in a country. For example, when the Berlin Wall came down and the Soviet Union collapsed, many in the West saw it as a great opportunity to do the evangelical equivalent of the Oklahoma land rush, charging in with Conestoga wagons full of Bibles. It was a knee-jerk reaction to a problem we thought God ought to be fixing, through us. The results of that foray are mixed at best. The Russian Orthodox Church—which, by the way, has had the Bible for at least a thousand years—pushed back, working with the Russian government to create a highly restrictive religious freedom law in that country. The results of that legislation have made things far worse for the Christian today than they were ten years ago.

AND THE EVIL THEREOF . . .

We can be even more horrifyingly specific about the nature of the world today. Toward the end of the twentieth century we saw the widespread use of the child soldier. This practice of making children into warriors employs a combination of hatred, fear and intimidation. Young boys are forced to cross the line of morality through an initiation process, which normally involves a killing. Once across that psychological line, it is very, very difficult for these children to go back. The child soldier is usually totally traumatized, is normally kept high on drugs and is placed in situations of personal vulnerability, namely armed conflicts. Today these soldiers populate many of the regional wars taking place around the globe. Sadly there is no one more ruthless, or less predictable, than the child soldier.

Another example: in the war in Bosnia that dominated the mid-1990s, women were specifically recruited to be snipers, primarily because they had more patience than men. They would be positioned in the hills around Sarajevo and would fire not on soldiers but on civilians. When innocent civilians—adults or children—cautiously appeared outside their own homes, there was a good chance that a woman would squeeze a shot off and bring a life to an end.

Earlier I mentioned the tragedy of the Rwandan genocide. Stories abound of impossible choices—of a man, for example, pleading that his children not be dismembered once dead and being given the "opportunity" to throw his family alive into a deep well, thereby granting his request.

One last example: World Vision was working in Chad when we encountered a young woman who had given birth to twins in the midst of a terrible famine. The famine was so great and the woman's condition so vulnerable that she realized early on that she could not keep both children alive. Like Meryl Streep's character in the movie *Sophie's Choice,* the mother had to make an agonizing decision. When World Vision arrived, that choice had already been made, and it was irreparable. One of the children appeared to be well fed, alert, even happy. The other was gaunt, sallow, vomiting and soon to die. I suppose we all have our own definitions of abject poverty, but for me people are poor when they are forced to make choices that preclude ethical considerations, actions that are forced from the very heart of darkness.

The statistics, the issues, the specific images do indeed favor the inclinations of the pessimist. The factual data is clear: this is a most difficult world that we have chosen to engage. The collective weight of that data suggests intractability. However, for those of us who believe in the sovereignty of God, intractability is not an option. Indeed intractability must be an offense to God's very being. In Scripture we see the rhetorical question asked over and over again: "Is anything too hard for the Lord?" The answer, which is obvious to the biblical writers, is a resounding no. Our Lord is the One who has the ability to change the course of rivers and the hearts of kings (see Proverbs 21:2). All power and authority are his!

We need not despair, but we do need to be wise concerning the workings of our world. With that in mind, Bosnia and Sudan are two examples where this collective data challenges the possibilities of ultimate success. This is where we find out how relevant we are and whether or not we have any answers to a world spinning out of control.

BOSNIA: THE ULTIMATE IDENTITY WAR

I am reminded of my friend Peter Kuzmič, a theologian from the former Yugoslavia, as he commented on that wonderfully hopeful period after 1989—when the walls came down, when statues of Lenin were placed in the horizontal position, when communism was pronounced dead.

"The Berlin Wall came down," said Peter, "and it fell on Bosnia!" Bosnia certainly took the celebration out of the end of the Cold War.

A brief history (sacrificing immense complexity in the interest of brevity) is appropriate here. The breakup of Yugoslavia in the early part of the 1990s plunged the Balkans into war. The driving force was the fear of having minority status in a potentially hostile environment. Catholic Croats, Orthodox Serbs and Bosnian Muslims—all of whom were afraid of becoming the vulnerable minority in a region rife with fifty years of ethnic tensions barely papered over after World War II— became the principal players in what would become a hostile and horrific environment.

The weapon of choice in Bosnia was ethnic cleansing. One side would go through a community and "cleanse" out all the people who were undesirable. For three and a half years, these battle lines went back and forth. Indeed some of the villages in Bosnia were ethnically cleansed more than once. The destruction was terrible and widespread. On a number of trips I personally toured many of these villages and was overwhelmed by the amount of destruction. I witnessed villages and towns that looked like Berlin after World War II—total rubble—except there was no air war over Bosnia!

These years of unspeakable descent into a moral hell, together with the promise of yet another long, cold winter, finally produced enough fatigue to bring the parties to the peace table. These talks took place in Dayton, Ohio, and became known as the Dayton Accords. Some have called them a peace agreement, but the accords really were nothing more than a pragmatic deal once the warfare had run out of steam.

Lines were drawn on a map that, in essence, cartographically ratified the cruel effectiveness of ethnic cleansing. The Serbs got something. The Bosnians got something. The Croats got something. Obviously this is a very tenuous peace. It certainly was not a just peace, and there is no way that anyone can argue that it was a just war. Unfortunately such a peace could lead to other unjust wars. But the reality and the pragmatism of the day were such that nobody wanted to fight any longer. An international force continues to hold together a fragile peace years after the cessation of the worst kinds of atrocities imaginable.

Why did the wars in Bosnia happen? What are the underlying causes, and what speaks to helpful principles of reconciliation? Let me mention just three of the causes. First, there was hatred and fear—hatred at the top belonging to a few that was translated into fear for many. I am not a psychologist, and I can't tell you what was in the mind of Slobodan Milosevic as he led his part of the world into four separate wars. He has finally been taken to The Hague, is standing trial before an international tribunal and may finally learn one of humanity's painful lessons: sin has consequences. During the wars, there was absolutely no question that this was a man who knew how to manipulate people and to instill fear in populations. Ultimately this combination of hatred and fear impacted the way people saw themselves, because their primary identity was formed by both ethnicity and religious belief.

Second, there was a history unforgiven. One could argue that the start of the Balkan War was announced in 1987 when Milosevic went to Kosovo and gave an extremely nationalistic speech about the "Field of Blackbirds," a Serbian defeat that is pivotal in forming the nation's identity. The Serbs have not had many victories in their long history, and they have had a tendency to glorify their defeats. The fact is, however, that this defeat took place in 1389! And now was their chance to get even. History unforgiven.

How does an unforgiven history work? David Manuel, author of *Bosnia: Hope in the Ashes,* provides an eloquent example of this sad reality. He reflects on a building that was flattened during the war. Gunners continued to pour round after round of artillery into an apartment until absolutely nothing was left. The building had housed only civilians, individuals who had really never done anything to those firing the artillery shells. To the question "Why destroy them?" we are presented the following rationale:

> Listen, you can't afford to think of them as individuals. They're
> the enemy—all of them. They deserve what they are getting.
>
> Why?
>
> Because of what they did to us in the past.
>
> How far in the past?
>
> During the war.
>
> Which war?
>
> The Second World War. They had concentration camps, too,
> you know; we did not invent genocide.
>
> But you weren't even alive then.
>
> That's all right, I heard about it.
>
> Where will it end?
>
> Not with me.
>
> When this is over, what will you have accomplished?
>
> When this is over, our people will be safe and we will have what
> we need.
>
> Is it right to take from another?
>
> They did it to us and they would again if they could.[3]

History unforgiven—a sad, perpetual cycle of revenge.

A third characteristic of this conflict, one that we will take up in greater detail in chapter three, is the challenge of the "other." Put differently, it is the challenge of moving from tenuous coexistence to principled pluralism, a legitimate diversity that comes from ethnicity and religion. In many parts of the world, of course, diversity is lifted up, considered a strength and celebrated by people who respect differences.

But in Bosnia, the home of different races, creeds and historical backgrounds, more than 200,000 innocent people would be killed because of a total lack of respect for this kind of pluralism.

More than fifty thousand Muslim women were raped during this conflict. The use of rape had little to do with sexual gratification. It was power designed to create shame, to destroy the dignity of another person and to leave survivors with massive trauma. The men were killed so they would never fight again. The women were traumatized so they would forget, or would be unable to speak about, what happened. And most tragically, in many cases the children were killed so they would not come back and exact revenge in the future. Once again, we see the wicked extremes of self-preservation: no one wants to be a minority in a hostile environment, so you do it to them before they do it to you.

This incredibly complex and horrific conflict ultimately assumed a human face. We were allowed to see on our televisions what Slavenka Drakulic wrote about in *The Balkan Express: Fragments from the Other Side of War:*

> After a year of violence, with the dead numbering approximately 200,000, with many more wounded and over 2 million refugees flooding Europe, there came a story of the concentration camps.
>
> On the cover of one of the weekly magazines, I think it was *Newsweek,* they had this picture of an emaciated, desperate man behind barbed wire. You could count his ribs and all his bones. All of a sudden, in this person behind the barbed wire, the world recognized not a Muslim but a human being. That picture, the words concentration camp and holocaust, finally translated the true meaning of ethnic cleansing. At last people in the West began to grasp what was going on. It was suddenly clear that Europe had not learned the lesson that history always repeats itself.
>
> Someone is always a Jew. Once the concept of otherness takes root, the unimaginable becomes possible.[4]

We said "never again" and yet the concept of otherness keeps rearing its head—and not just in the Balkans.

. . . AND THE ONGOING INTRACTABILITY OF SUDAN

One can forgive the secular world for seeing these conflicts as intractable. They defy description and they defy easy solution. I was reminded of all of this when the incident of a government bombing of an elementary school in southern Sudan in early 2000 came to light. I was working in the State Department at the time as Ambassador-at-Large for International Religious Freedom. Sudan was one of the first, and easiest, countries to designate and sanction because of its widespread abuse of religious freedom. The predominantly Muslim north imposed Shari'iah Law, an act totally unacceptable to southern Sudanese, who are mainly Christians and animists. Nor did it help that the north is Arab and the south is African. Adding to the complexity, oil was discovered primarily in the south, but is now being extracted by the government in Khartoum. In short, here was yet another country that could numb the mind with its complexities.

The school was located in the Nuba Mountains. A group of first-graders was meeting under a tree, next to the school, when the Khartoum government dropped bombs on the area from high in the sky. Seventeen children were killed. They were in the midst of an English lesson when these bombs literally blew their unsuspecting bodies apart. To compound the horrific nature of this tragedy, a senior diplomat representing the Khartoum government out of Nairobi made this audacious statement to the international community: "Yes, we intentionally targeted that school."

Bishop Max Gassis has given most of his life to children. He is the Episcopal bishop working in the Nuba Mountains who built the school. Right after the bombing, he came to the United States, beseeching our government to do something, anything, to preclude this kind of tragedy from ever happening again. I met with him and then made arrangements for him to meet with my boss, Secretary of State Madeleine Albright.

Max came in one afternoon and told the Secretary his story again. He told it with all the pain and all the emotion that comes from someone who could identify every one of those seventeen first-graders. The Secretary was very moved, and when the meeting ended she took me into her office. "What are we going to do? How are we going to fix this?" she asked with a great deal of frustration in her voice. She was beside herself because there was not an easy answer. The situation in southern Sudan was, and remains, very difficult to "fix." There is not much global interest in the country from the standpoint of the West. Unlike Kosovo, there is no "NATO equivalent," no coalition of interested countries to go in and right wrongs.

At the time of my conversation with Secretary Albright, the conflict in Sudan was already nearly two decades old. I remember my sense of impotence as I said to her, "Madam Secretary, if it were easy it would have been fixed seventeen years ago." Today, with a new source of revenue fueling the conflict—the rich oil fields under government control—it is obvious that more time will elapse before we see the end of the carnage in the Sudan. This is all part of the nature of our world.

HUMBLING OPPORTUNITIES

It is just these mind-numbing, searing, paralyzing events that push the world to find solutions in unconventional places. A few years ago the number-two man in the Pentagon, the Undersecretary of Defense, invited my pastor, a young Presbyterian minister, to lunch at the Pentagon. When the minister got there he saw that he was surrounded by a number of high-ranking military officers—resplendent in deeply starched uniforms and rows of ribbons for achieving successful solutions to past problems—eagerly awaiting this "audience" with a pastor. They sat down for lunch, dispensed very quickly with the small talk and then made clear the real reason for the unusual gathering.

One of the attendees was a Navy admiral who was about to become the commanding officer of the Seventh Fleet. This command extended throughout the Mediterranean and covered all of the Balkans as well, including the latest unsolvable problem of the day, Kosovo. He spoke first: "Tell us about reconciliation. Specifically tell us about forgiveness. We are seeing things in Kosovo that we have never seen before." Amazing! America, the last remaining superpower, and its Pentagon, one of the great symbols of global power, had taken this day to ask a young pastor to come and talk about reconciliation. It is refreshing that a meeting like this could occur in Washington, and the image of this consultation should be painted prominently on our consciousness.

What a time to speak truth to power! Here was an opportunity to speak on something so fundamental to the Christian faith and so important to creating sustainable solutions to complex humanitarian issues. Reconciliation—the heart of our gospel. And forgiveness—essential to the process, methodology and spirituality of reconciliation. Instead of a briefing on geopolitics, the military professionals that day were briefed on grace—grace all sufficient, grace that abounds and allows for forgiveness more powerful than even these sinful, horrific crime scenes from around the globe.

I do not know the lasting effects of this meeting. What I do know is that there are more opportunities for the church today than in any time in the history of our faith. The world has run out of answers. It appears there is nothing that can be done. And so a person of faith is brought in, a Christian worldview is given a hearing and a contribution is made that can have far-reaching impact.

As the composition of conflict changes and we engage in more and more of these intranational "identity" wars, the role of religion and faith will be increasingly important. This is especially true in those conflicts where our entrance has been based on a moral imperative. Think about it. Why did we attack Serbia during the conflict in Kosovo in 1999? It was a sovereign nation. The respect for national sovereignty is something that goes all the way back to the Peace of Westphalia in 1648. Why was NATO so aggressive about that small sovereign country? The answer is very simple: NATO, with the strong presence of the United States, bombed Serbia because there are some things that transcend the sovereignty of a state. In this instance it was very clearly the sanctity of human life in Kosovo.

Why would the United States think of going into Somalia in the early 1990s? This was certainly not a piece of territory America needed. We weren't looking for warm-water ports for our naval battle groups. As far as anyone can tell, there is not a thimbleful of oil to be had in that country. No, America went into Somalia because at the time the Marines landed there, 75 percent of the children under five were starving to death. And any country that cannot protect the majority of its own children does not deserve the right—has not earned the right—to call itself a sovereign nation. Once again, the sanctity of life was more important than the sovereignty of a state. Certainly Christians understand that God's will trumps humanity's flawed efforts in political theorizing about sovereignty. There will be countless opportunities to use both the message and the methodologies of our faith in helping to resolve some of these protracted conflicts.

Governments can do things that are not in the purview of any other entity. They can negotiate treaties. They can enforce them. They can provide resources for binding agreements. However, governments cannot change human relationships. Human relationships are not negotiated; they are reconciled. And this is where the powers that be will turn to

Christians who wish to be credible and relevant.

FACES IN THE DANCE

We spent a great deal of time in this chapter talking about statistics, issues and major conflicts, which provide a context for discussing today's realities. This context, however, has a human face. And on that face there exists the potential for an incredible amount of hope.

I close the chapter with just one example. On our last trip for World Vision in 1998, Margaret Ann and I went to Lebanon. Lebanon had just lessened travel restrictions imposed during the long and bloody civil war that transpired there, a conflict that took more than 140,000 lives.

While in Lebanon, we met a young woman named Mary and learned about the day that changed her life. A militia group had come into her village and began to shoot at anything and everything that moved. Instant panic set in and people began to run, bodies began to fall and, as you can imagine, there was total chaos. Mary ran as well, but she tripped. Before she could get up, a young man from the attacking militia came to her and, knowing that she was a Christian, put a revolver to her head and demanded, "Renounce the cross or die." Mary was eighteen. There was much about life that she did not know, much that was yet to be revealed. But she was absolutely sure about her faith. "I'm a Christian. I was born a Christian, and I will die a Christian."

The revolver exploded in her face. The bullet went into the left side of her chin and came out the base of her neck. On its way, it shattered her spine. Instantly and irreparably Mary became a quadriplegic. The young man then took out his bayonet, carved a cross on her chest and left her for dead.

The next day the militia realized they had a very practical problem on their hands. They had decided to stay in the village, live there and take it over completely, but to do that they would have to do something about

44

the people they had killed the day before. There were piles of bodies around the village that were beginning to swell and stink. The militia came to one large group of about thirty bodies, where many of Mary's extended family lay dead. In the middle of that mass of human carnage, they heard a soft groan. Miraculously Mary was still alive. Just as miraculously, the militia took her to the local hospital.

We were sitting with Mary in a home run by the Catholic Church in Lebanon, and I found myself shaking my head. "Mary, that doesn't make sense at all. Why in the world would they try to kill you one day and take you to a hospital the next?" Mary has one of the most disarming looks I've ever encountered—totally serene, transcendent—and a demeanor that shows she has long since been reconciled with her world. She responded softly, "Sometimes God uses evil people to do good things." I found this unsatisfactory. "Mary," I asked, "how about the person who did this to you? How about that young man who tried to blow your head off and only succeeded in getting you confined for the rest of your life in a wheelchair?" Again the soft reply: "I've already forgiven him. I hope he is alive because I would like to forgive him face to face someday."

Think on this: an Arab woman held hostage by her own body, living out her life in a wheelchair in an institution. She is paralyzed in a land that, at that time, was twice occupied—by the Israelis in the south and the Syrians everyplace else—and somehow she has the ability to transcend all of that.

I tried a final time: "You mean you are going to forgive the person who pulled the trigger. Why would you do that?" Mary's answer is equally sure: "I forgave that person because that is what my God did for me."

Far from being wasted in her most promising youth and now finding herself strapped to a wheelchair of despair, Mary is a reconciled person who knows from where her hopes originate and how she, in turn, can most appropriately use the baton of reconciliation that has been passed to her. She is one of the writers of the new rules. Mary has done something we all can do. She has positioned herself to bear witness, to suggest—indeed, to live out—a solution to the evils of our world. Mary has become the incarnational presence of the message of reconciliation. She has adopted the "mind of Christ" and has become the very presence of Christ in a difficult world.

Mary is a witness. She is a witness to the incredible love of a heavenly Father who would spare no expense, not even his Son, to make sure we have access to him. A seat at his table!

Mary is more than credible: she is relevant. She is having a profound impact on everyone with whom she comes in contact. Her life speaks volumes. Her witness is just as sure as that of a young eighteen-year-old girl looking at death and realizing who she is and to whom she belongs.

Mary is down on the dance floor, wheelchair and all. She is repeating the story of our Lord's redemption. And she is doing a superb job of it. In the midst of all that's intractable, in a world of terrible hurts, Mary stands out like a bright light revealing why the news is good. She is a manifestation of hope that is tangible—one that each of us is capable of providing.

3

DIVERSITY

Embracing the Other Among Us

The piety, charity, and simple gestures of friendship of [the monks'] Muslim neighbors represented both a challenge and a confirmation of their own faith. Muslim hospitality toward them had been an invitation to renew their commitment to live the Gospels daily. Wasn't the friendliness of so many of the Muslims with whom they lived a clear sign of the workings of the Holy Spirit, the spirit of fellowship that is at the heart of all men? God's love for man is echoed in His desire for men to love one another. Can't all God's children reveal something of God, each in their own way? How to break out of the horrible errors of the past, when men despised and killed one another in the name of their religion? Isn't the greatest obstacle to peace man's rejection of those who are different?

JOHN W. KISER, *THE MONKS OF TIBHIRINE*

Slavenka Drakulic wrote, "Someone is always a Jew. Once the concept of otherness takes root, the unimaginable becomes possible." There are no more sobering words than these as we begin the twenty-first century. Diversity is not celebrated. It is denigrated to the point that whole people groups can be demonized, excluded and, in all too many cases, exterminated. At the end of World War II, the collective consciousness of the world screamed, "Never again!" Unfortunately the past decade has exposed a shortness of memory. The mindless genocide of Rwanda, the slow burn of Burundi and the ethnic cleansing in Bosnia and the Nuba Mountains of Sudan—all speak to the most extreme forms of exclusion, over and over again.

Legitimate differences, such as ethnicity and religion, form the basis of much of our identity. But instead of celebrating differences, we now have in our lexicon *identity wars*—those intranational conflicts implemented along the fault lines of primary identities. It is impossible to understand our world today without an appreciation of this most difficult challenge: how to embrace the *other* in our midst.

IDENTITY: HERE'S WHAT IT LOOKS LIKE

Otherness refers to the identity of the other that leads to exclusion. During one of my trips to Bosnia in the mid-1990s, our driver one day was a Croatian named Mario, whose wife was expecting their first child in a few months. "What are you going to name your child?" I asked. His reply said much about the culture in that part of the world, for better or for worse. "If it's a boy, I only have two choices: either the name of my father or my grandfather. It's expected of the firstborn. I can't break the tradition. It's been that way for a thousand years."

Mario was loyal to tradition. After all, this was part of who he was. It was his identity and, in the Balkan states, identity means everything. A last name will distinguish the Croat from the Bosnian, a Bosnian from a Serb. The alphabet used to spell the names will also discriminate. Croats use the Latin alphabet, while Serbs follow the older Cyrillic form.

Spiritual expressions serve to differentiate as well. A Catholic Croat will cross himself with two fingers, moving left to right. An Orthodox Serb will make the sign of the cross right to left, using three fingers. Catholics build their churches on a north-south axis. The Orthodox construct theirs east-west. Even without a sense of direction, however, one could easily distinguish the differences based on domes, spires and minarets.

And then there are the rooflines of the older homes. A Croat will construct his or her home with a single gable roofline. The Muslim's roof will come from four different sides, emerging as a single point at the top. It is all part of registering identity, and it is all taken very, very seriously.

As I suggested previously, the war in Bosnia was all about identity. Such wars are intranational, taking place within national borders. The conflict, then, has very little to do with nationalism or citizenship. It has a great deal to do with identity and with fear—and even acute paranoia—especially if your identity is in the minority. Again, no one wants to be a minority in a hostile environment. Cleanse the other identity from your midst! Diversity is not to be celebrated; it is to be feared. The tools of discrimination are employed: names, alphabets, crosses, traditions and even rooflines.

This is the new tribalism that emerged at the close of the twentieth century. Some have argued that the next war will take place between civilizations, not nations. Unfortunately Bosnia helped to make that case. East meets west. Muslims battle Christians. A protracted identity conflict prepares the soil for major conflagration. Remember: "Once the concept of otherness takes root, the unimaginable becomes possible."

SEEKING IDENTITY

It is always unfortunate when an identity is established at the expense of someone else. Such an exercise also speaks of personal weakness. There is a story told about the Soviet Union in the late 1980s, as the walls were coming down and the Russian empire was crumbling. One of Mikhail Gorbachev's deputies said to his interlocutor on the American side, "You're going to miss us. You will miss us because now you will have to define yourself in terms of what you are for, not in terms of what you have been against."

It was relatively easy for the United States to have an identity that was developed and energized by what it was against. The Soviet Union was the "evil empire." For forty years America had the "luxury" of having an enemy, a focal point and a foil for its own explanation. Since that was taken away, America has had to self-define. This has not been an easy exercise. Sadly it was easier to create identity against something than to speak to the world those values and principles on which America stands.

This has been one of the problems in writing the new rules of international affairs generally and of America's international role specifically. By any explanation, the last decade has to be seen as one of greatest opportunity for what some have called "the last superpower." But recent history suggests more struggle than success, more floundering than foundational strength, more second-guessing than single-mindedness. America's national interests continue to be defined by military security and global economic penetration.

Military and trade interests are obviously important, but neither really speaks to our best instincts and highest values. The moral imperative is sometimes hard to find in our global decision making. Indeed it is most often left out of our definitions of national interests. We are far from consistent in our implementation of human rights. We fail to appreciate that, although the "hard" issues (trade and security) can be negotiated by good people, the "soft" issues that surround human dignity and sanctity of life are ones that people continue to die for. America is groping for a way to constructively represent the fundamental identity of the American experience and its people.

Christians appear to have this same problem constructing an identity. At the risk of oversimplification, there appear to be two ways Christians define themselves. One group begins with what they are "for." Their starting point and the center they work from is Jesus Christ, "the author and perfecter of our faith" (Hebrews 12:2). From that center, they can draw their circles wide. And from that profound position of strength, they draw circles to include. In contrast are those Christians who define themselves by taking the center of the circle for granted while they seem to be more concerned with the issues at the circumference. This group tends to define itself by the things that it is "against." Quite naturally then, we find a number of litmus tests on the circumference of the circle. Depending on how well you do on the circumference, this group decides whether you are "inside" or "outside" the circle of fellowship.

The issue of identity, and the very real question of whether we will respect someone whose identity is different from our own, has profound implications for our lives at many levels: the relevance of our Christian witness, the ability of a country to demonstrate effective leadership in the world and, ultimately, the ease by which the unimaginable can become possible.

EXCLUSION: HOW IT HAPPENS

How does it happen, the creation of the other in our midst? I am indebted here to the work of John Paul Lederach, an expert on reconciliation theory and a practitioner who has spent the major portion of his life working in some of the most difficult contexts in the world. I especially like his faithfulness to the biblical text and the logic of Scripture as he implements the specifics of reconciliation methodologies. He suggests three factors that are prominent in the creation of enemies: separation, superiority and dehumanization.[1]

Separation. Obviously there are many ways to separate, to exclude. We separate from others when we focus on our differences instead of what we share in common. (We will talk more about this in later chapters.) When we only focus on differences, we violate a key principle of the reconciliation exercise, namely the search for commonality. Make no mistake about it: we choose where we want to place our focus. The optimists, those who construct their faith from the strength of the center, will always focus on common elements.

In the mid-1980s, a number of Americans were kidnapped in Lebanon over a couple of years. The first one taken was the CNN bureau chief in Beirut, Jerry Levin. Jerry was nominally Jewish—agnostic to a fault. During the next eleven months, while chained to a radiator, Jerry would become a Christian. He eventually escaped, or was released (no one is ever quite sure how these things happen), and would go on to become an outspoken advocate for the Palestinian cause, in spite of that awful incarceration by Arab extremists.

Jerry worked for World Vision during my own tenure there. We talked a great deal about his kidnapping and about how someone who was victimized by a group of people could then become such a strong advocate for the larger group they sought to represent. Obviously Jerry speaks with a great deal of credibility on this issue of separation. "If we only have 2 percent in common," he once said to me, "we need to work on that 2 percent. If we begin there, and are faithful in our focus on those things that we share in common, I'm convinced that there will come a time when we will see a great deal more that holds us together."

Separation and exclusion can be done very subtly. For example, in international parlance it is politically correct to use the word *tolerance*. This word appears in all the international covenants related to human rights and, in general, speaks to a "live and let live" approach to people who might be different. Personally I have never liked the word. To me, tolerance is a weak form of grace applied to someone I do not especially care for. "I do not really like you, but I will tolerate you." Tolerance suggests a difference that I have to accommodate, apart from my normal inclination and perhaps from my better judgment. A better word, and a word that breaks down the walls of separation, is *respect*. Respect speaks to a common celebration not simply of our diversity but also of something much higher: our commonality as people created in the image of God.

We also separate from our common humanity when we create a personal identity at the expense of someone else. Miroslav Volf, a Croatian by birth and a superb theologian, has written a great deal on this issue of exclusion. Speaking of separation, he says, "Instead of reconfiguring myself to make space for the other, I seek to reshape the other into who I want her to be in order that in relation to her I may be who I want to be."[2] This form of separation can be observed in spousal relationships. It may be subtle, it may be unintentional, but it can quickly become a destructive reality in the relationship between a husband and wife. It sounds something like this: "I would like my wife/husband to be predictably this and that so that I will be allowed to be less predictable whenever I want."

In short, we want to create our identity and make it stand out. Unfortunately all too often this only happens at the diminishment of those closest to us. At one level, such an exercise represents the height of arrogance. At another level, it also demonstrates the depth of cowardliness. Ultimately we exclude people by robbing them of a part of their identity.

Of course, Christians have multiple points of connectivity, even across major denominational lines. We share a similar faith, a major aspect of our commonality. Together with that faith, we share the same hopes. And we share a portion of that same love that flows from our Lord and Savior.

It is not nearly as easy, however, to connect at a point of suffering. The biblical text reminds us that "if one part suffers, every part suffers with it" (1 Corinthians 12:26), but connecting at this point of deepest need is not easy.

Today more than 200 million Christians are being persecuted because of their faith. The vast majority of this persecution, in which Christians are being kidnapped, driven from their homes, raped, beaten, tortured and murdered, takes place outside the United States. Nonetheless it is persecution occurring inside the divine circle drawn for the body of Christ.

How is it that we have such a difficult time relating to Christians in Laos, for example, a number of whom are spending the day in leg irons because they refuse to renounce their faith? Why were we so silent as a church body when it was time to reconcile the country of Vietnam with the United States? Why did the worldwide fellowship of believers seem to be absent during the darkest days of the Rwandan genocide? We need to see this as part of the problem of separation. Our inability to relate to and connect with a suffering world comes at the expense of the unity of the body of Christ. Whether or not it is the size of our country, the strength of our affluence, the increasing ability to shut out those things that make us uncomfortable, this kind of separation diminishes our witness as Christians.

Superiority. We also push people away and exclude them when we see ourselves as superior to them. A superiority complex is nothing more than an enhanced judgment about ourselves and, by extension, a deprecatory judgment about others. It is also true that a person who has arrived at such judgments probably suffers from the problem of triumphalism as well. This is not a good place to be! It is the incarnation in reverse, an example of ethnocentrism—all too common to many aid organizations based in the West—that erodes the best of our intentions.

Paul's letter to the church of Philippi contains some of the most beautiful incarnation language in Scripture. He suggests that our attitude should be the same as our Lord's,

> who, being in the very nature of God, did not consider equality with God something to be grasped, but made himself nothing, taking the very nature of a servant, being made in human likeness. And being found in appearance as a man, he humbled himself and became obedient to death—even death on a cross! (Philippians 2:6-8)

Now, that is a model and a methodology that will lead us to embrace our fellow human being! This is the attitude we must develop to counteract a superiority complex and the judgments that ensue from it. Would that it could be part of our reality. All too often, if we are candid about such things, we find ourselves in the same situation as James and John, the two sons of Zebedee, who came to Jesus inquiring about their future status, each one wanting to be positioned next to our Lord. What a disappointment this must have been to Jesus. It was not only an anti-kingdom impulse, it was also working against the model of the King himself. In short, it went against everything Jesus was teaching the disciples at the time.

"Who is going to be greatest among us in heaven?" Jesus took this example of inherent pride and addressed it this way: "Unless you change and become like little children, you will never enter the kingdom of heaven" (Matthew 18:1, 3). What a great metaphor! Most children do not have complexes, neither of superiority nor of judgment. Children will not judge or suggest that they are better than you. And children do not drive people away; they draw people.

The analogue at the national level is the superiority complex called imperialism. Colonization has had a long and tortured history simply because, at its base, it is built upon a national complex of superiority, one nation over another. Likewise, to a large degree, the creation of reservations for Native Americans was a consequence of a superiority complex held by the majority of Americans.

Even today our residential neighborhoods are separated on the basis of social and economic class. Consider the gated community and the slum. This is not a point that needs to be pushed very hard, but suffice it to say, we still have the ability today to separate on an elitist perception of self.

Dehumanization. We also can create the other through the process of dehumanization. History has shown that we have the ability to desecrate that which is considered sacred: human dignity and the sanctity of life. What principle was at work in the raping of all those Muslim women in Bosnia? It was not as much about sexually degrading women (though that was important) as about dehumanizing them. Once they were desecrated, they would think of themselves as less than they should, and control over them would be made absolute in the most negative way.

We also have a tendency to underestimate how easy it is to justify injustice and violence via the perverse logic of dehumanization. We console ourselves by imagining it is only unsophisticated miscreants who indulge in cycles of dehumanization. The entire war in the Balkans was written off: "It's not us—we wouldn't do that. It's those other people, those non-European savages." But we used the term *savages* in our own country's history, justifying the killing of so many Native Americans. Hitler followed a similar principle to destroy more than six million people. Once people are thought to be inferior and incapable of a positive contribution to majority populations, they are separated, denigrated and dehumanized. The record of history has shown that once such a creation of the other takes place, the unimaginable does become possible.

Make no mistake about it: there is a massive price to pay for excluding the other in our midst, for constructing an enemy and for destroying human community in this way. Volf captures these consequences as he speaks to this core issue after a decade of identity wars:

> Ethnic otherness is filth that must be washed away from the ethnic body, pollution that threatens the ecology of the ethnic space. The others will be rounded up in concentration camps, killed and shoved into mass graves, or driven out; monuments of their cultural and religious identity will be destroyed, inscriptions of their collective memories erased; the places of their habitation will be plundered and then burned and bulldozed. For those driven out,

no return will be possible. The land will belong exclusively to those who have driven the others out—out of their collective construction of themselves as well as out of the land. People of pure "blood" and pure "culture" will live in a land that has been cleansed of the others. A company of political, military, and academic "janitors of the ethnic household" will employ their communicational, martial, and intellectual mops, hoses, and scrapers to re-sanitize the "ethnic self" and rearrange its proper space. The result: a world without the other. The price: rivers of blood and tears. The gain: except for the bulging pocketbooks of warlords and war profiteers, only losses, on all sides.[3]

These are strong, and strongly appropriate, words. Volf goes on to look at three additional sets of exclusionary factors: assimilation, domination and abandonment.

Assimilation. Assimilation is based on the principle that the other needs to become like us. The only way one might become more like us is to let go of some part of his or her own identity. Assimilation, then, comes at the expense of identity.

When I was president of Eastern Baptist Theological Seminary in the mid-1980s, we saw a major influx of Hispanic students to a seminary that historically had been largely Anglo. We talked a great deal during those days about the proper assimilation of these students into a culture that had been created by Anglos. As you might imagine, our Hispanic colleagues were very much concerned that they were going to lose something of themselves. The metaphor *melting pot,* for example, produced both anger and fear. Fortunately they convinced the rest of us that the richness of diversity contains a great deal more value than some forced homogenization of the present environment.

Similarly there is an entire house church movement in China that is reluctant, to say the least, to be assimilated into the governing structure of China's ruling authority. Millions of Christians attend these churches, sometimes known as the underground church, which are growing rapidly. The Communist Party of China has made them illegal, and still they grow. It's hard to know whether this growth phenomenon is a result of persecution or whether the persecution by the Chinese communists is a result of the growth.

Regardless, the Communist Party would very much like to assimilate the house churches into the existing governmental structure for churches, the Three Self Church. Three Self churches register with the government, and all their activity must be cleared by the government, including worship times, worship places and, in some cases, even the sermons that will be preached. For example, in a Three Self church, it is possible that you will never hear a sermon on the second coming of Christ. To communists, such talk is apocalyptic—and it scares the dickens out of them! The Communist Party continues to go to great lengths to make the Three Self Church the only Protestant church in China. For most of the house fellowships, however, joining the Three Self Church would be a destructive assimilation, something that would erode the distinctness of a holistic Christian identity.

Next door in Vietnam, a similar situation exists. House churches are illegal and have been harassed actively for the better part of the past twenty-five years. One recent change, however, was the registration of the Tin Lahn Church, a fellowship started by the Christian and Missionary Alliance in the south of Vietnam with about 250 congregations at present. In April 2001, Vietnam registered this denomination, the first Protestant one registered since the end of the Vietnam War in 1975. This caused a great deal of angst among many of the faithful congregants of the Tin Lahn Church. On the one hand, the church was looking for a legal identity, a legal relationship with the government that would protect them and the way they had chosen to worship. On the other hand, they were very concerned about giving away too much of their core identity. Attempting to "render unto Caesar the things that are Caesar's and unto God the things that are God's" takes a great deal of discernment, especially in a communist country.

The first constitution written by the leaders of the Tin Lahn Church appeared to bend over backward to appease the government of Vietnam. A massive uproar ensued, led by those pastors who had been growing their house churches under the great persecution of the last twenty-five years. Eventually a constitution was written that the church could support and, most interesting, the party elites went along with it. Implementation is still something that will be watched keenly, but the hope is that the proper balance between the secular and the sacred was achieved.

Volf has a marvelous summation of the principle of assimilation: "We will not vomit you out if you let us swallow you up."[4] In other words, "If you let us assimilate you, we will let you live and have an identity." But, of course, this is no longer an identity. In many parts of the world, assimilation as a methodology of control is very, very real.

Domination. Domination can also be a form of exclusion. If you are the one with the power, you also have the power to exclude people from your group, from your business, from your circle of friends. Slobodan Milosevic had power. He used that power to take his country to war on four occasions in a decade, excluding people through his primary weapon of choice: ethnic cleansing.

Saddam Hussein had power—an amazingly resilient form of power. One might think we had dropped enough bombs on him to rob him of his ability to dominate. But after the Gulf War, we gave him an economic out, namely the ability to produce for sale a certain number of barrels of oil a day, with the understanding that the proceeds would go to making his people less vulnerable. In short, he had oil to sell so he could feed the children and provide medicine to the populace. But instead of support for the whole Iraqi population, spectacular palaces were built to satisfy the ego needs of a dictator. The money was used to dominate the other, whether the other was the Shiites, who were being destroyed systematically in the south, or the Kurds, who were being gassed in the north, or closer to home, the innocent citizens of Iraq, who were denied basic food and medicine.

In the same Middle East region, we see dominance by one of our allies, Israel. There is only so much water to be had in the region, and Israel has been very effective at dominating the supply. Much of the modern highway system in Israel has been built without on and off ramps to key Palestinian villages—again, a form of domination. In Jerusalem today, more and more Palestinians are being forced from their homes while, at the same time, there is an ever-increasing number of concentric circles of building around the city—building exclusively for Israelis. Because of the purported need for construction and the fact that America has largely bankrolled much of these efforts, the domination of a people continues unabated.

Another example of dominance is prevalent in Romania. There are two basic faith groups there—Orthodox and Reformed—which have been warring silently for centuries. If you happen to be an Orthodox kid walking home from school, you may have kids from the Reformed Church throw rocks at you. And if it is the other way around, you may find some Orthodox rocks raining down on your head. Interestingly, however, if you are a gypsy, the Orthodox and the Reformed will stop throwing rocks at one another and join forces in throwing rocks at you. A gypsy gets it from both sides—domination.

Abandonment. The third exclusionary factor is abandonment. Here metaphor and reality become the same—that is, we abandon the inner city for the safe suburbs; we retreat from the dance floor to the balcony. Unlike the good Samaritan, we continue to cross over to the other side of the road. In the name of security, we establish the gated community.

There are all kinds of ways to abandon something. This is a genera-tion that has grown up with a remote in its hand, a remote with a mute button. In Gujarat, India, forty thousand members of the human race die in an earthquake, but if it is too difficult for us to watch, we can switch the channel. If we do not want to hear the cries of the dispossessed, the downhearted and the downtrodden, we can shut off those cries.

We do the same to countries. It has been virtually impossible to draw the attention of the world to the plight of the southern Sudanese. Their cry for help has gone on for at least twenty years, and some might say ever since independence was declared from Great Britain in 1956. Still they remain a distant people somehow different from us, a wearisome problem that seems never to go away. And so we shut them out of our minds.

Over the past several years, my wife and I have been increasingly in-volved in Laos and have come to love the Laotian people. We have even developed a little sympathy for the Laotian government. Part of my own fascination with Laos stems from the time when I was part of a so-called secret war on that nation in the 1960s and early 1970s. Twenty-five of the three hundred combat missions I flew in Southeast Asia were flown "secretly" over Laos. We dropped bombs there because the trans-portation system for war supplies coming into South Vietnam was es-tablished there.

After the war, there was no longer any use for the elaborate system of trails that flowed through Laos. Goods could be brought more cheaply over the now peaceful South China Sea. There was no reason to take the longer, more difficult route. Once that happened, no one thought of Laos anymore.

Today most of the region gets a lot of attention from the business community—but not Laos. Why should anyone look specifically at

Laos? There are only 5 million people. Vietnam has 85 million, China 1.3 billion. The economic community can pass Laos by because there are not enough cheap manufacturers or future consumers.

From time to time countries will take abandonment on the chin. However, the worst thing imaginable is when vulnerable individuals are intentionally abandoned. I was able to see a lot of things during my eleven years as president of World Vision. One of the worst was a Home for the Unrecoverables in Romania in the early 1990s. This was a place designed for any child who had something medically wrong with her or him that the government, through its broken medical system, could not fix. This meant that a child with a cleft palate, for example, could end up in one. A child who experienced bed-wetting could go there as well. Once there, the children stayed until they died. Nothing would be healed or cured once they arrived, so whatever the malady, it would only get worse. The Home for the Unrecoverable, then, was where people sent their young ones to die.

The home we visited was about fifty miles from the city of Iasi (pronounced *yosh*). We were traveling on a beautiful fall day through gorgeous countryside. We drove into a small town, and at the end of one of the streets on the outskirts of it we saw the simple cement-block home. Although every conceivable malady seemed to be represented there, most of the children were still very young. There were three to four babies in every crib. At best, each child received three "touches" a day: one diaper change and two meals. The rest was all self-stimulation. The babies would rock back and forth in their cribs, banging their heads against the sides as they sat together on their urine-soaked mattresses. The older children were not much different. Although this was a rather cool day in the fall, many of the teenage kids were naked, collected in various parts of a room, rocking back and forth, banging their heads against the walls for stimulation or perhaps attention that never came.

We were warned by one of our colleagues going in: "This will be difficult. Look at the children's eyes. They will help you." It was as if the children knew that we were seeing painful things, that the abandonment of human dignity is the most terrifying form of exclusion. They did try to help us and would smile back at us, in spite of their pain, in spite of their filthy conditions, in spite of the awkward silence in which we could only stare. The place stank and the kids stank.

When a child got extremely sick and was near death, a worker would take that child down and put him or her in the basement. There the child would stay until death overwhelmed the fragility of life. Someone from the staff would go down every night to see if there were any dead bodies. The dead children were taken outside and, if it was summer and the ground was easily managed, a shallow grave would be the final resting place. If it was the dead of winter and the ground was frozen, the dead body would simply be laid outside. Dogs and other marauding animals of the night would then do the work of the shovel.

This is a European country, the so-called civilized part of the world—and this all took place within the past ten years. What this says to me is that the issues of abandonment and exclusion are still present. There is nothing far-fetched about abandonment! Sadly, dozens of such orphanages continue to exist, and this tragic abandonment continues to be a major exclusionary methodology in the twenty-first century.

EXCLUSION: WHY DO WE DO IT?

Why do we exclude? Many times our tendency toward exclusion is based on *fear*. And fear grows exponentially the closer an issue comes into our own space. "Homes for troubled teens are fine," we insist, "just don't build them in our backyard." "Yes, there comes a time when sex offenders should be let out of jail. But please don't release them into my community." The closer the fear, the higher the wall we are capable of creating.

As I have already suggested on a number of occasions, *hatred* also plays a major role in our tendency toward exclusion. What motivates a skinhead? Why does the Ku Klux Klan still command its sympathizers? Hatred can initiate many a fight and fuel many a conflict. History demonstrates that it goes hand in hand with fear.

Sometimes people exclude out of *indifference*. This is perhaps the cruelest cut of all. It is more than simply not taking the other seriously. The other is made to feel without value when ignored by someone who is part of his or her life. It could be someone of the opposite sex, a parent, a sibling, a boss or a professional colleague. Indifference might be encased in superficial niceties, but it produces something far short of a relationship of meaning. One can maintain indifference for a long, long time. It is the easiest exclusionary methodology to sustain, and one of the most difficult and despairing to overcome.

Embrace: What We Can Do About It

Much of this chapter has been spent on exclusion, the negative aspect of creating the "enemy" in our midst. There are ways to avoid it, however. The following four approaches, taken collectively, are methodologies I have seen create positive relationships time and time again. They are proven ways of enhancing the identity of the other and embracing people as legitimate friends.

Acknowledging that all are created in God's image. "Created in God's image"—the words are so familiar to many of us that we take this thought for granted. It might be the most profound aspect of all creation, however. And it is as mysterious as it is divine. Humanity portrays God's workmanship! Humanity bears the stamp of our Father Creator.

Think of the story of Jacob. After decades of estrangement from a defrauded brother, Jacob is brought back into the presence of Esau. It has been years since he schemed against his brother, stole his birthright and then ran when Esau threatened to kill him. As the two brothers approach one another, Jacob feels the same fear that drove him away in the first place. But the fear proves to be unfounded. The impossible becomes a reality: the two brothers are reconciled. Jacob, overjoyed, captures all of the emotions of the day with the acclamation, "To see your face is like seeing the face of God" (Genesis 33:10).

Jacob was allowed to remember that each of us is created in God's image. Each of us has eyes that are capable of seeing "the face of God." This is the great common denominator. This is also the rationale for inclusion. There is something in each of us that is representative of our Lord.

Knowing others by name. Names are important. Calling someone by name will demonstrate to the other some knowledge of his or her distinctive identity. Adam and Eve got to name all the animals, an exercise that was more than dominion; it was steeped in respect toward the recipients of those names. A first-year medical student is asked to memorize all the names of the various bones, muscles and nerve groups of the human anatomy. Someone has said that the beginning of wisdom is calling something by its proper name, and the naming exercise is the foundational step toward the practice of good medicine.

Anonymity is often deeply implicated in the worst horrors of human behavior. The Romanian orphan who is dying is not only moved to a different part of the facility; his or her name is taken off the bed—a sign that the person has been diminished, discounted and soon will be forgotten.

In the late 1980s, Margaret Ann and I were in Ethiopia together. It was a critical time for us to be there. Ethiopia was between famines—the major famine that was so destructive in the mid-1980s and the next famine that appeared ready to begin in the fall of 1987. I needed to make the case to the American people that what we thought we had fixed was still with us. It was not an easy marketing exercise.

Specifically I was looking for a strong metaphor to explain this dynamic to people who could respond with help. We were working out of a dusty little village named Agibar, a couple of hundred miles north of the capital of Addis. During our time there, I was off being "presidential" while my wife was out and about truly engaged in ministry.

Margaret Ann came across an old woman who had collapsed in tears and despair. Slowly the woman began to tell her story. She had entered the past famine full of life and love for her family. She had eight children and, as the famine grew increasingly severe, they began to die. Seven of her eight children would die during the Great Ethiopian Famine. Someone once said that starvation is a death by inches. This woman experienced a great many inches.

At the end of the famine, her husband, who was weakened and sick in one of the camps, also came to a premature death. Now she was left with one child, and the hunger in her stomach was a constant reminder of the ravishments still fresh in her mind.

Agibar is a feeding station where people come to get their monthly allotment of food. This woman made the trek from her small village, received a large bag of food, placed the bag down by a tree and went off to get help to carry it home. When she returned, the food was gone. She had lost her food, the hunger was still there, and it would be another month before she could receive a second allotment. No one understood the vulnerability of her situation better than she.

Margaret Ann quickly fixed the situation. She took the woman to the head of the line and got her a second allotment of food. The woman's tears receded. She gave Margaret Ann a look of pure gratitude and slowly trudged off toward her village.

When Margaret Ann told me the story, I was elated. I had found my metaphor! This was what was happening to the people of Agibar and, by extension, people throughout Ethiopia. They had already been decimated by a famine, in many cases losing virtually everything, and they were now extremely vulnerable. There was no surplus left, no body fat that would take them through the next season. They had already killed their animals. Their crops could not be gathered. In many cases like this old woman's, they had already lost most of their family. Now a second famine was about to hit and they were hungry again.

I came home from Ethiopia and wrote about this metaphor I'd found on the eve of yet another disaster. I sent my notes to my colleagues in World Vision, and it was quickly followed by a disturbing admonition from the head of World Vision, Great Britain. He said, "Bob, that was a great story, a great metaphor, but you never told us her name."

I knew immediately what he was saying. And it was very convicting. Was this woman simply a metaphor, a marketing scheme that could be employed back home, a way to raise money from all the fat cats in the States? People have names, faces, pulses and personalities. Had I denigrated this woman unintentionally by knowing so much about her and yet not even knowing her name?

We went back and found out her name. Her name is Sintayas. At the time she was only 56 years old, but through the pain of famine and the destruction of family, she looked much, much older. She had indeed lost everything. She was well aware of what hunger could do and she was about to experience it all over again. She was vulnerable, and in a very real way, I contributed to that vulnerability through my failure to call her by name. Even with the best of intentions, it is still very easy to exclude people if we do not allow them the simple dignity of acknowledging them through their most basic identity, their names.

Realizing everyone can contribute. We need to realize that everyone has something to contribute; everyone has something to offer to the well-being of those around them. In the early 1990s, I went to a special kind of orphanage in the town of Cluj in northern Romania.

Every child there had something terribly wrong with him or her. Every one had a debilitating physical handicap. The handicaps were less than benign. These children's bodies were broken when their parents attempted to abort them before birth. The attempts failed in killing them but succeeded in irreparably destroying any hope of physical wholeness.

But the physical impairments were not the last shot to the children. Because they were less than perfect—blind, deaf, crippled, limbless—they were the first to go to the orphanages. And without the benefit of professional help, their mental capacities began to diminish. Limited human touch and the absence of human love take an immediate toll on a child's developmental process.

Our eyes and feelings tried to absorb this human landscape. These children represented brokenness. Though they were created in the image of God, they were fashioned in the image of sin. They were victims of the total collapse of respect for human sanctity and dignity.

Early in our visit, one of the boys came up to me, tugged on my sleeve and asked me in perfect English, "Do you love Jesus?" I initially thought it was a scam to play into the hearts and emotions of those from the resource-rich West. But it wasn't. The director of the orphanage was a Christian who taught his charges about Christianity and taught them to speak English. The orphanage's rooms and hallways were all decorated with Bible story pictures. As I began to look at these pictures, I realized how totally and completely our Lord was represented in this orphanage.

"Do you love Jesus?" Of all the things this boy could have been curious about—justice, fairness, pain, why bad things happen to good people—he simply wanted to know if we shared this one thing: the love of Jesus. I have been a Christian all of my life—churched, Bible camped, youth grouped and Sunday schooled—and this was the only time I can remember when this question was so directly and personally put to me.

"Do you love Jesus?" "Yes," we replied. And why not? He is the One who allowed these children to have a childhood. He is the One who nurtured from within, when the whole world seemed to be arrayed against their external appearance. He is the One who made himself known to deformed children, loving them "before the foundation of the world" (Ephesians 1:4 NRSV). He is the One who gives each of us hope—hope that transcends the brokenness of our world.

This was the question that Jesus put to Peter before the ascension. "Peter, do you love me? I am expecting you to do big things, Peter—feed my sheep, take care of my lambs, be watchfully engaged with my children. You are going to make a great contribution, Peter, but I need to know first whether or not you love me. Peter, this is important. The commandment to love is always given before the commission to go."

That little boy in the orphanage at Cluj had the same insights, knew enough to ask the same question and was making that day an immense contribution to my sense of priorities. The most profound theological question ever asked was coming from an orphan who almost did not get to be born.

We avoid the inclination toward a negative view of the other when we realize that each has a unique contribution to make. Scripture says, "Do not forget to entertain strangers, for by so doing some people have entertained angels without knowing it" (Hebrews 13:2). My young friend was an angelic gift to me that day.

Becoming friends. The final way we can avoid excluding the other is by intentionally turning that person into a friend. A year after my 1988 visit to Hanoi, I had occasion to return to central Vietnam, specifically Danang, where I had been stationed for thirteen months in the late 1960s. This was a great adventure for me. We were flying into Danang over familiar landscape, landing on a runway I had taken off and landed on more than three hundred times before, rolling down the runway past landmarks that brought poignant memories.

As we landed, my old hangar came into view. It was a little shabby, sporting a great deal more rust than I remembered, and the surrounding area was much overgrown. But it was still unmistakably my hangar. The foxhole to the left of the hangar was still there, marked by a low mound that obscured most of the underground facility. This was where we would run when the rockets began to rain down on the airbase.

The revetments that were built to protect our aircraft from these same rocket attacks were also still there. Instead of our A-6 Intruders, however, the revetments now held Soviet-built MiG-21s. Admittedly this produced a strange feeling. I have always described the Vietnam War as a war that neither side won or lost, producing victims on all sides. Seeing a squadron of MiG-21s where American planes used to be certainly made the point that we did not finish first.

I wanted to go over to my old hangar. I wanted to take that memory walk to where I had spent such a significant time of my life. I wanted pictures. And I needed permission. All the officials I talked to promised they would look into my request, but no one was able to do anything about it.

Finally I was taken to the office of the commander of the airbase. We sat across from one another, separated by a table. I made my case to him, explaining my desire to return to my old hanger. He actually delighted in repeatedly turning down my requests. It was obvious that he continued to see me as the enemy, and he wanted to make very sure I realized his side had won. In 1972, the American forces withdrew in what would eventuate in a massive defeat for the South a few years later. This commander wanted to reenact that defeat, if only metaphorically, by displaying his superiority over me.

I found myself arguing with him. I was extremely frustrated, very angry, and there was no other place I could go. The base commander was not helpful at all. Sometime during the early part of this conversation, he told me that he flew MiG-19s out of Hanoi during the war and had shot down a number of American planes. During my first three weeks in Vietnam, we had lost two airplanes from my squadron, and I had lost two roommates. My blood was now boiling. I felt obliged to say to him, "And I dropped over 1700 tons of bombs on your people." At this point, no one would accuse us of being very good neighbors!

Finally, about twenty minutes into the argument, he surprised me with a question: "Do you have any children?" I paused a moment and said, "Yes, how about you?" He replied that his eldest son was about to graduate from college as a chemical engineer. I told him about our eldest, Chris, who was soon to graduate from Stanford in International Relations.

I could feel the level of animosity falling. For the next several minutes, we talked about our families and our hopes for our children. We were no longer fighting one another. We were like a couple of old veterans telling war stories, reminding each other of our hopes that our children would not have to do what we had done, namely go to war.

I forgot about my desire to see my old hangar. As the meeting came to an end, however, the base commander stood up and walked around the table, that table with all of its history, emotion, pain and wasted years. He did something unique for any Vietnamese person, much less a base commander: he gave me a huge, spontaneous bear hug. Then he said to me, "Come with me, I'll take you to your hangar."

Be careful whom you learn to hate. Be careful whom you exclude. Be very careful whom you make to be the other in your midst. You may become friends! In fact, if you want to destroy your enemy, make him or her your friend.

IDENTITY AS CHRISTIANS

One final thought. This issue of identity should be especially real to the Christian. Our Lord and Savior, Jesus Christ, knew a great deal about identity. The theme is both powerful and persistent with him. He claimed to exist before Abraham. He told his disciples he was one with the Father. He announced his kingdom and left no doubt that the King and the kingdom are one and the same. During his trial before the crucifixion, one of the few times he spoke was when his identity was questioned. He was asked, "Are you really the Christ?" This question was directed at Christ's identity but, by extension, his very authority was also being questioned. For him, the identity was sure, the answer positive—and the crucifixion quickly followed. Jesus would rather die than compromise his divinity. Just as important, he could embrace death because of that divinity. This is the identity that makes him distinctly different.

As a supreme act of grace, Christ's identity has become ours: "We are heirs—heirs of God and co-heirs with Christ" (Romans 8:17). We share the same family tree. We come out of the same traditions. The God of history and the Christ of Calvary are related—and they are related to us!

Let me summarize. We see the sacred dignity of each person, because each has been created in God's image. We include the other by remembering their names, because those names already have been written on the palms of his hands. We take seriously their contribution because every good and perfect gift comes from the Lord. And finally, we truly love our neighbor, even if she or he started that day as an enemy, because God first loved us.

Yes, "someone is always a Jew." Hopefully, in a positive sense, that will always be true. To help ensure the best of our diversity, however, each of us needs to be capable of a giant bear hug, a fitting embrace for the other in our midst.

WHAT WE'RE ABOUT

4

TRUTH

Hacking at the Root

One word of truth outweighs the entire "world."

ALEXANDER SOLZHENITSYN

My initial visit back to Danang, Vietnam, continues to be an unforgettable experience. It was not the most pleasant conversation that I have ever had, but it was certainly one of the most memorable. There were two very significant points reached in the course of that conversation. They each say much about the process of reconciliation, and it will be helpful for us to unpack that incident in a little more detail.

The first turning point occurred when the base commander told me what he had done during the war: "I flew MiG-19s out of Hanoi. I shot down American airplanes." As I had lost friends and roommates over North Vietnam at that time, I hoped my response was just as stinging: "And I dropped over 1,700 tons of bombs on your people."

We were both speaking out of crude, raw emotion: anger, hurt, pride, triumphalism—there was enough here to set civilization back a few centuries! But in a more positive sense, we were engaged in the act of truth telling. We were relaying to each other what we had done that was harmful and caused pain to the other. The tone of that discussion notwithstanding, we were confessing our pasts, laying out the specifics of those activities that were so harmful to others. We may not have been at the place of repentance at this point in the conversation, but confessing needs a subject and an object, and we certainly had both.

This is what people do when they look back on their lives, see the negatives and choose to break free from a difficult past. The only way this is remotely possible is when we tell each other the truth about that past. If there is no truth, there can never be repentance. And if there is no repentance, it is much more difficult to experience mercy, or forgiveness, which is so important to a more positive future.

The second turning point in that conversation was when the commander asked me about my family. This began a long discussion around a subject we had in common and about the future each one of us hoped our families would experience.

In the process of reconciliation, we always need to find a point of commonality, a point that we own together, a point that can move us forward. Moving forward means changing the negative narrative of the past, healing the memories of that past and coming to a new place where a more positive future comes into view. Talking about our families gave us both a starting point: the future became more important than the past.

I firmly believe that finding that point of commonality is nothing short of a profound moment of grace. We will talk at length about grace in the following chapter, but it should be noted at this point that one does not always tell the truth and one does not always find something in common with one's enemy unless there is a nudge of the Spirit.

So truth telling is looking backward. Defining a point of commonality is a launching pad into the future. In our dialogue, the base commander and I faced difficult and troubled pasts but a most hopeful and preferred future. The one confessed, the other articulated, and when we rose from that table with all of the junk of the past twenty years, the bear hug was genuine and enemies became friends.

A PROFOUND IMAGE FOR RECONCILIATION

As we begin to get into the specifics of reconciliation, it would be helpful to lay out the logical flow of the next several chapters. Some years ago, John Paul Lederach pointed me toward Psalm 85:10 as an image for reconciliation. The verse is as poetic as it is meaningful: "When truth and mercy embrace, and justice and peace kiss." John Paul was working in Latin America, trying to affect this difficult exercise of reconciliation between two very conflicted parties. Psalm 85:10 was used as a devotional, and each morning he would discuss in depth each one of these components: truth, mercy, justice, peace.

The question was finally asked, "What happens when all these components are in place?" "Oh, that is easy," came the reply, "then you have reconciliation!" That may sound simplistic, but I have spent a great deal of time over the last several years looking at these components in light of global realities, and I am more and more convinced that each one of these is indispensable to a right relationship.

These four components—truth, mercy, justice, peace—are the core of the reconciliation process. As we look at each component, it will be obvious that reconciliation is more than a process; it is also a spirituality. Grace and mercy take this exercise to a higher place. That thought alone makes it necessary for Christians to be at the forefront of such a process.

These are also components that attest to the difficulty of the task. Truth telling—confessing the sins of the past and repenting of what we have done that has caused so much pain—is a difficult starting point. Mercy, that combination of forgiveness and grace that seeks to forgive the past, is certainly not any easier. Truth telling and mercy together are absolutely essential, however, if we are going to be honest about where we have been and have any hope for a different reality in the future. Justice and peace speak to the future. Justice means, among other things, that sin has consequence. King David confessed his sin, and the Lord forgave him, but the consequence of his sin was that his kingdom was never the same. And finally, there is peace, which needs to translate into security for all parties, a new reality and a future that is both positive and secured.

This brief description using Psalm 85:10 should at the very least suggest that the process of reconciliation is not for the faint-hearted. This is long, hard, difficult, frustrating work. If it were easy, would Christ have had to go through the agony of Gethsemane and the pain and humiliation of Calvary? Reconciliation is the heart of the gospel, however, and where we need to be most engaged.

One other caveat as we begin to unpack these components: we should not look at the reconciliation process as linear. I have already hinted that the nudge of grace allowed for truth telling to take place between my former enemy and me. Grace is the fuel that energizes this process, that makes it more a spirituality than a mere secular exercise. And often it is the prompt of grace at the point of mercy and forgiveness that allows the other components of truth, justice and peace to have a ghost of a chance.

THE MOST DIFFICULT WORDS

The most difficult thing you will ever have to say to someone is "I'm sorry." Now, some people might find this an easy exercise. They are able to get things off their chest very quickly. Others may have an easy time apologizing because their words are meaningless. But if we look back on tough conversations, we remember that we had done something wrong and knew that confession and repentance were necessary. We swallowed hard, exposed our identity, our self-esteem and our ego, and said, "You know, I did this and I am sorry." In those arguments, the nudge of grace was both very real and very necessary.

Let us return to truth telling. How do we arrive at truth? How do we, to quote Henry David Thoreau, strike at the root as opposed to "hacking at the leaves of evil"? Pontius Pilate seemed to be concerned about truth, but it turns out that he was blinded by it. Pilate undoubtedly fits James's description of a double-minded man trying to appease all sides and losing the truth that was standing right in front of him. The result was predictable: Pilate allowed truth to be crucified on the cross.

What is the real truth in the Balkans, that convoluted concoction of ethnicity, religion, history and conflict? This is a difficult question. Today there are three different histories being written about the last several years: one by the Bosnian Muslims, one by the Croatian Catholics and one by the Orthodox Serbs. So much for pluralism! Imagine how destructive these different stories will be to any further attempts at reconciliation. At this point, there is no agreement whatsoever on a common reality or truth about the past. Instead today's children are being presented with three different perspectives of what really happened in their young lives. This inability to tell one another the truth will have a profoundly negative impact on how these children will deal with their future.

In the Middle East, truth has been equally elusive. Both Israelis and Palestinians have written textbooks that do not acknowledge their enemy neighbors. Each is trying to create a perception of reality—a perception woefully lacking in truth telling. This is a recipe for disaster.

It is obvious that the futures of the Palestinians and the Israelis are inextricably linked. Israel needs its security guaranteed just as much as the Palestinians need economic viability. Those two needs must be met, together. Unfortunately there has been a missing element in every attempted peace process. Photo-ops and obligatory handshakes notwithstanding, what these two longtime antagonists have yet to do is to tell each other the truth about the past. Israel needs to say: "This is what I did to you. In 1948 I came in and bulldozed your homes; I tore up your olive trees; I took your land; and I made refugees of your people." Similarly the Palestinian must tell the truth: "This is what I did to you: I denied your existence; I dedicated myself to your destruction; I sacrificed my children and my children's children on the altar of revenge." Until this exchange happens, there is simply no hope that this long-running conflict will be any closer to a positive conclusion. Those who would attempt to bypass this exercise will prove as ineffective as those who call, "Peace, peace" when there is no peace (see Jeremiah 6:14).

TRUTH, THE FIRST CASUALTY

Let's turn to an example in which an individual had difficulty telling the truth. President Clinton went on national television to make the announcement, "I did not have sexual relations with that woman." While surrounded by applauding but unknowing friends, the president had very intentionally set truth aside. Ultimately, after three years of parsed phrases, three years of syntactical gymnastics, three years of lawyers who were laboring over what the word *is* really means, the combination of a stained dress and the threat of prosecution forced truth to emerge.

What a terrible ordeal to put the country through, all because telling the truth was too difficult. We found out that the ethical standards of this president were tied not to morality but rather to what the legal system could bear. It was fitting, then, and oh so sad, that as the president left town at the end of his tenure, a lawyer standing behind a bank of microphones told the world that a deal made to preclude prosecution after office still did not mean that the president had really lied.

This is the problem when we choose a course other than truth telling: the lies get easier to tell. But in this long and sordid episode, a perjury did take place. And as anyone who has ever worked in the Justice Department will tell you, perjury has to be punished. If not, our entire justice system falls apart.

Truth is elusive. It has sometimes been called the first casualty of war. That is not always immediately obvious for those of us who have served in a war. From an individual point of view, war may be the most honest environment in which we participate. When the first shot is fired in anger, we react. If there is bravery, it shows. If there is cowardice, it shows. If there is foolishness, that will be seen as well. It is impossible to disguise oneself in the middle of a conflict.

There were individuals in my squadron who had been in the service for ten or fifteen years but had never been in a war before. By the time of the Vietnam War, they were relatively advanced in rank and had a number of service medals pinned to their chests. They were the "old salts," but I watched some of them become very different people when raw, paralyzing, legitimate fear was injected into their environment. All of the façades picked up over many years can be stripped away in one chilling moment of fear. War is a very honest and truthful environment for the individual.

But institutionally truth becomes an early casualty in war. In early 1968, the Commandant of the Marine Corps came to Danang for a visit, and I was asked to be a member of the briefing team. A colonel called me aside and suggested, "Tell him about the MiGs you encountered over Hanoi." I answered him, "Well, you know, I never really encountered any MiGs myself." He quickly replied with a note of consternation in his voice, "Well, somebody encountered them, so you are the person that needs to talk about them." He added another subject: "Make sure you tell the Commandant about evasive maneuvers when multiple surface-to-air missiles were sent your way." Again I found myself obliged to reply, "I never had any more than a single surface-to-air missile come my way at one time." He was having a hard time making his point. "Yes, but there were other people who must have had SAMs shot at them in multiple configurations. Tell them about that."

That briefing, and the not-so-subtle shift from what was factually correct, became a microcosm of the entire war. As the war went on, sometimes supported by little lies and sometimes by a total absence of truth, we lost faith in reality. We lost that faith because no one had the courage to tell the truth. I will never forget that confident phrase of General William Westmoreland, commander of the entire U.S. military operation in Vietnam: "I see the light at the end of the tunnel." That remark came just six weeks before the Tet Offensive of early 1968, which placed the entire allied force on the defensive. It was now only a matter of time before we would leave. So much for the light at the end of the tunnel!

Truth is also the first casualty in politics. At the end of the Bush-Gore debates in the 2000 presidential election, CNN produced what they called a "truth squad." They would devote time after each debate to highlighting the things Bush said that were not totally true, followed by the untruths spoken by Gore. How sad that in a country that loves its democracy we need to have such "truth squads."

Truth has proven to be elusive throughout government. A major exercise in government is putting together talking points around a particular subject. In the State Department, hours upon hours are devoted to defining difficult issues through a series of talking points. The talking points are then sent up the ranks for further refinement. If a particular talking point would put at risk a single vote, it was often eliminated. There is no other way to say it: at the end of the day, a political overlay trivialized truth. Issues could not stand on their own merits; they had to support the administration in power. Is it any wonder that our culture creates television programs like *Spin City* and *The Spin Room?* We witness a daily parade of party leaders spinning the events of the day into our living rooms, each one giving his or her take on the "truth" of an issue and producing disillusionment and disgust among the audience.

I think the ultimate indictment of my generation will be that we produced great politicians and virtually no leaders. Let there be no mistake, there is a difference! You cannot be a leader without truth, without a passion for truth, without accepting it regardless of where it takes you. The politician can follow the polling data and discern which way the wind is blowing on a particular issue. The leader does not have this luxury. Legitimate leadership is anchored by what is true.

There is a memorable line in *A Few Good Men,* spat out of the mouth of Jack Nicholson in full Marine Corps dress to a junior officer, played by Tom Cruise: "You can't handle the truth!" Well, the fact is we can handle the truth. We should not be diminished or disrespected by people lying to us. We can take unvarnished truth. This is something we can handle.

Truth always bests the lie. Accepting reality always beats existing in some artificially contrived world. Without truth, there can be no trust; without trust, we have lost the major building block of a civil society. Just imagine if King David, or King Nixon, or King Clinton had told the truth, or at least came clean early on. Their country might have forgiven them. They could have gone on with their tenures; they could have had their full agendas dealt with. But they intentionally chose to distance themselves from truth and from that divine spark of grace that would have allowed truth to be a platform for a much better future.

Indeed nothing good ever happens when truth is removed from the human equation. The biblical examples are many. Cain denies knowledge of Abel's fate and is reduced to refugee status for the rest of his life. Abraham tries to pass Sarah off as his sister and only succeeds in diminishing her as his wife. Jacob fabricates (literally!) the person of Esau in front of his semi-blind father and is absent from their fellowship for the next twenty years. Using a lie, David positions Uriah the Hittite in the front lines, and his kingdom never fully recovers. Truth is obviously very important to our Lord. Those who violate it do so at considerable peril.

TRUTH'S SILENT PARTNER

If truth is so important, how might it be enabled? How do we encourage the process of truth telling? How do we draw people back again to what the Old Testament metaphorically refers to as "the plumb line," to the moral compass, to "those ancient guideposts" of truth? How do we protect our self-esteem, our relationships, our professional bonds and our sacred trusts from our inability to speak truth? There is no limit to the amount of grace necessary to get us through this step. One of the most liberating verses in all of Scripture is when Paul reminds us, "Where sin increased, grace increased all the more" (Romans 5:20). Grace is always stronger than sin. It always exists in larger quantities. It is the silent partner but the strongest member in the spirituality of reconciliation. It prompts truth, allows for mercy, ensures justice and delivers peace.

Grace is also the force that connects us with God. In the history of humanity, its presence is indisputable. Look, for example, at the first dozen chapters of the book of Genesis. In incident after incident, there is an explosion of grace. For example, the world initially is "formless and empty" and "darkness was over the surface of the deep" (Genesis 1:2). God penetrates that darkness. He overcomes the chaotic formlessness of nature and creates a perfect universe.

Adam and Eve opt for the apple and, for the first time, feel the shame of their nakedness. The Bible says that God covered them with the skins of animals. Those skins had to come from the shedding of blood—the first sacrifice—and grace was applied to original sin.

Cain excludes his brother permanently: he kills him. The motive was anger and a bruised ego, a difference in the acceptance of one offering over another, a difference with which Cain could not deal. He takes his brother out into a field and bashes in his brains. There is a call to justice as God demands of Cain, "What have you done?" The sin has consequence: Cain is now a fugitive. But there is also grace. He will be protected by a mark on his forehead.

There came a time when the Lord was grieved at the depth of human sin, even regretting that he had placed us on Earth. Justice required punishment. The sin and the punishment would destroy the world as it was then known, "but Noah found favor in the eyes of the LORD" (Genesis 6:8). A vehicle was created to preserve the future of the world.

In an attempt to make a name for themselves, a group of people begins to construct a tower that will reach to heaven. The Lord is highly displeased and prescribes a monstrous punishment. The Tower of Babel may be taking shape, but God is removing a common language. What a gift was lost! But out of that judgment, out of the tribes that formed and the nations that developed, one nation is called forth through which God would make himself known to the peoples of the world. And this is what he does through Abraham, an immense act of enabling grace in the midst of a sinful world.

Reconciliation would end in early despair if it were not for the massive prompts of grace that keep the process going. It is grace that allows us to include, allows us to embrace. It is a gift—God's gift toward us. It is a spiritual gift—one of the reasons reconciliation is more than a strategy; it is a spirituality performed by people. We have not created the gift. Indeed most of what we have done works in opposition to this marvelous infusion of grace. God's grace continues to be stronger than our sin.

Some months after the Rwandan genocide, a member of our World Vision staff was riding with his driver through the streets of Kigali, Rwanda's capital. They came to a busy intersection and were stopped at a red traffic light. A young man ran out of the crowd and knocked frantically on the window next to the driver. As soon as he got the driver's attention he gushed out the words, "I am sorry," and then ran off, disappearing back into the crowd. The driver dissolved in tears. Our staff member was obviously a bit bewildered and asked, "What's going on?" The driver collected himself and then spoke softly, "That's the person who killed my parents."

Truth telling. There is nothing very neat about it. It can emerge from a shouting match between two former enemies or it can be the plaintive cry of an overwrought sinner, delivered through an automobile window at a busy intersection. How does this happen? What brings us to the point of repenting, of feeling that the truth we carry is simply too painful to live with? I would suggest to you that it is the prompt of grace that begins the process. There are no shortcuts to this component of truth telling. Eventually it has to happen. There is nothing worse than a past papered over, a life of unconfessed sin, a denial of the reality that is ours. Gratefully, our Lord promises an infusion of grace, grace sufficient, grace more abounding than all the collective messiness of our broken and hurting world.

5

MERCY

Forgiveness, Forgetting and Divine Memory Lapses

Forgetting the suffering is better than remembering it, because wholeness
is better than brokenness, the communion of love better than the distance
of suspicion, harmony better than disharmony. We remember now in order that we may forget then; and we will forget then in order that we may
love without reservation. Though we would be unwise to drop the shield
of memory from our hands before the dawn of the new age, we may be
able to move it cautiously to the side by opening our arms to embrace the
other, even the former enemy.

MIROSLAV VOLF

Truth is difficult, but forgiveness is the hardest act that any one of us
will ever have to perform. Miroslov Volf sees forgiveness as the point of
ultimate demarcation, the boundary between exclusion (sin) and embrace (reconciliation). Dietrich Bonhoeffer actually saw it as a form of
suffering, where we "consciously deny a rightful claim to justice." Os
Guinness envisions forgiveness on a continuum between Eric Segal's
trivialization, "Love means never having to say you're sorry," and Win-
ston Churchill's comments on Lenin, "Implacable vengeance rising from
a frozen pity. His sympathies cold and wide as the Arctic Ocean. His ha-
treds tight as the hangman's noose!"

This raises an early question for you to ponder as you read this chapter. We have heard about cheap grace, but when does forgiveness become cheap as well? In our global context today, when does cheap forgiveness begin to appease, and even encourage, evil?

Truth keeps the process of reconciliation from becoming abstract. What keeps forgiveness from doing the same? A statement I heard some years ago continues to burn in my mind: "Truth without love is aggressive; love without truth is mere sentimentality." How much mercy do we apply to truth? How much love is needed to generate forgiveness? How strong a prompt of grace will be required to get us through the difficulties created in our past?

Make no mistake: forgiveness is not just a difficult decision. We also can get its implementation very wrong. I would love to have a dollar for every time I've found myself in need of my wife's forgiveness and tried to gain that forgiveness prematurely. On many occasions my timing to be forgiven and her timing for making that happen were not the same. When this happens we have the potential of pushing the process of reconciliation backward, sometimes even causing more pain than the original offense. There is always much to consider when forgiveness is an intentional part of the package: timing, emphasis, faithfulness to facts (truth), consequences and perhaps even forgetting.

Then there is the Lord's Prayer, which suggests that our being forgiven is contingent on how we forgive others. Mercy is a conscious choice made tangible in the act of forgiveness and prompted by grace. Granted, that is a mouthful—but if reconciliation is the heart of the gospel, mercy is the heart of reconciliation.

MERCY PROMPTED BY GRACE

I have already suggested that the reconciliation process is nonlinear. Many times it begins with mercy. Perhaps the best example of this is Christ's prayer from the cross: "Father, forgive them, for they do not know what they are doing" (Luke 23:34). Certainly there is no confessional truth telling here. There has been no repentance offered. There is only the mercy of our Lord, prompted by grace, a forgiving-and-forgetting example that raises the bar and establishes the standard for reconciliation. Jürgen Moltmann acknowledges that raised bar:

> In the name of the crucified, from now on only forgiveness holds sway. Christianity that has the right to appeal to Him is a religion of reconciliation. To forgive those who have wronged one is an act of highest sovereignty and great inner freedom. In forgiving and reconciling, the victims are superior to the perpetrators and free themselves from compulsion to evil deeds.[1]

But the greatest mistake we can make is assuming that only the Divine is capable of this kind of mercy, that only Christ can pull it off. I think of our Lebanese friend, Mary, who is living out her life strapped to a wheelchair because she refused to renounce her faith. What is left, as we found out through a series of long discussions with her, is nothing short of forgiveness and mercy, a desire to meet her assailant face to face so she can tell him what she has already done, namely forgiven him.

I think of Gladys Staines and the missionary family from Australia who had spent over thirty years treating leprosy patients in India's hinterlands. One night in January 1999, her husband, Graham, and their two sons went to a distant village. Arriving late, they planned to sleep in the car and begin their services in the morning. Sometime around midnight, a gang of hostile adults surrounded the car and began to smash the windows with stones. As the two young sons huddled with their father inside, the mob set the car on fire. They were burned to death.

I was working at the State Department when this occurred, and my initial thought was that certainly Gladys and her daughter would return to Australia and live out their lives in grief. Amazingly that did not happen. In a very moving memorial to her family and the work they felt called to do, she forgave the ones who destroyed so much of her life and vowed to stay in India to continue the ministry. One of the most powerful stories being told in Orissa, India, today is the story of Gladys Staines and her ability to forgive.

And then this story, from a friend in Rwanda, Antoine Rutayisire, as he shares his inspiration for collecting testimonies of Christian bravery during the 1994 genocide:

Rosalie was brought in the church on crutches. Her face, and in fact her whole body, was still wrapped up in white bandages. Her neck was held in position by a special plaster collar. Wherever I looked at her, I felt deep pity.

Then in the middle of the service she stood up and asked if she, too, could give a short testimony. I was expecting a tirade of self-pity and accusations, a recounting of all the suffering and misery she had gone through. I expected her to want to arouse sympathy for herself and anger at the criminals who had reduced her to that state. But Rosalie astonished all of us by the positive praise she gave to the Lord. She told the assembly how the Interahamwe had captured her, had killed all her family, and then had cut her in all deadly places. They cut her temples, her neck, and all over the body. She was left to die on the border of the road. For three days she bled and suffered pain from the cuts, thirst and cold under the heavy rains. Finally she was found by the RPF soldiers who gave her first-aid treatment and then transferred her to the hospital.

She recounted her story in a factual manner, without any attempt to create emotional effect, and praising the Lord for every detail of her rescue. The conclusion was more powerful than the story. "I know all of the people who did this to me. They were our immediate neighbors. I spoke to them and they gave me time to pray for them before they started cutting me and I prayed for them until I lost consciousness. I forgave them before they did it and I still feel forgiveness for them. If I were to meet them even today, I would not hand them over to justice. I have forgiven them and I wish them well. I know it was the devil that led them to do such an abomination, and I pray the Lord to save their souls from perdition."[2]

These are examples of humanity, people created in the image of God, responding to the most heinous of deeds that have impacted their lives. Their response is one of forgiveness. Forgiveness, the application of mercy, breaks the cycle of evil and allows for a new narrative. At the very least, these examples clearly suggest that reconciliation is more than a process, more than a methodology and more than a strategy. Reconciliation is also a spirituality. This is why our Lord could talk so passionately about it.

Sunflowers and Prodigals

There are two stories that challenge our thinking as to the role and impact of mercy. One comes out of Simon Wiesenthal's horrific experience in the Nazi death camps of World War II. The second is a parable told by our Lord in response to the supposed doctrinal purity of Pharisees and lawyers.

Simon is living out what he thinks to be the last days of his life in a Nazi concentration camp. For the Nazi, the Jew was less than human, and that is the treatment Simon experiences during his captivity. One day he is "invited" to visit the bedside of a dying Nazi SS soldier in the hospital next to the camp. The soldier, whose name is Karl, is terribly wounded and knows he is dying. His last wish is to be able to speak to a Jew—as it turns out, any Jew—in order to confess to something he had been a part of during the war. Simon stands by Karl's bed and listens to his terrible tale. It involved the rounding up of Jews, forcing them into a common building, setting fire to the building and then, as they jumped from windows, shooting them until everyone was dead. The event weighs heavily on the soldier. He intimates that he even shot Jewish children.

But now Karl himself has been shot and mortally wounded. His time is short. Before he dies, he wants to have this sin in his life forgiven by a Jewish person. The confession is heard, forgiveness is asked, but it is more than Simon can bear. He leaves the soldier to die, without the forgiveness that was so much desired, because he does not feel he has the right to speak for the victims of Karl's crimes.

But did he do the right thing? Was there something else he could have done? Wiesenthal wrestles with these questions all his life and ultimately leaves that last question to us. In his book on the incident, *The Sunflower,* he invites others to add their own thoughts about what would have been the most appropriate response to Karl's last request. Among the commentators who responded to Simon's appeal for additional input, most of the Jewish writers agreed with his refusal to forgive. On the other hand, most of the Christian responses were biased in the direction of forgiveness. Perhaps this relates to the strong identity Jews have with suffering, and the equally strong emphasis that Christians have to a "grace-filled" theology.

There is some commonality in the pathos of the moment. Karl and Simon are both barely alive. A man about to die asks forgiveness from a man who has been, essentially, condemned to death. There are certainly strange goings-on at death's door. Interestingly this is not dissimilar to the exchange at Golgotha. The thief about to die turns to One also soon to be dead and asks for help. The thief wants to be remembered, but Karl wants Simon to "help me forget." The thief had a tremendous amount of faith; Karl had an overwhelming sense of guilt.

Karl asks for a "representative Jew." Simon was not seen as a person and neither were any of the victims of the Nazi terror seen as human. They were recognized only as Jews, a categorization that dehumanized the individual and, consequently, weakened the substance of Karl's confession.

Ultimately forgiveness was not extended, at least not verbally, but there were acts of grace made evident. Simon stayed alongside the bed and listened to the entire confession and thus honored the humanity of the other. At one point, Simon helped the wounded man drink water. At another place, he waved an annoying bug from Karl's face. It is obvious that human niceties were not yet made extinct in the camps. Simon's prolonged stay with Karl, as well as his quiet exit, were benevolent acts. By staying and listening, Simon gave comfort. But he did not forgive.

Indeed the hardest act that any one of us will ever perform is the act of forgiveness. What would we have done? Were the sins against Gladys Staines, Mary and Rosalie more difficult to forgive than those Simon Wiesenthal encountered? Are there sins best left unforgiven? What are we to do so that our forgiveness is not cheapened, so that we don't appease and encourage evil?

WHAT WOULD JESUS DO?

This brings us to our second story. The Pharisees always had answers for every question, a rule for every occasion. But this is where our Lord weighs in with a heavy dose of practical theology: the parable of the prodigal son. The context of the parable is formed by the specific criticism the Pharisees leveled at Jesus: "This man welcomes sinners and eats with them" (Luke 15:2). Jesus rises above rules and shares a parable that speaks to the transcendent nature of relationships. But along the way, since the Pharisees brought up sin, Jesus reminds them that he knows a great deal about the subject.

The parable is perhaps Christ's most famous, but I'd like to highlight the specifics that would speak most directly to the Pharisees' sense of sin. For starters, there is the premature request from the younger son for "my share of the estate" (Luke 15:12), essentially suggesting to the father, "Father, I wish you were dead." There is the forced liquidation of assets, the breaking up of the land, the dividing and hence diminishing of the family safety net. Ultimately we find the Jewish son consigned to the pork business, working for a Gentile. This becomes a self-inflicted identity conflict, a conscious act of exclusion and an immense embarrassment to the family.

Yes, Jesus understands sin! But as if the Pharisees need a more direct commentary, Jesus adds a postscript to the parable. There is the unforgiving elder brother, another prodigal, one who remains physically close but spiritually distant from the father. This is the one who replicates the pharisaical tendency to elevate rules over relationships. Parenthetically we should also recall here that two of Jesus' own disciples, Judas and Peter, were prodigals. There was a time when they became the "outsiders," when fellowship with Jesus and the other disciples was broken. Ultimately we are told that one went outside and wept bitterly. One went outside and hanged himself. Sadly not all prodigals return.

The elder brother is hard, unforgiving, suspicious, cynical—a resentful son who remains outside the celebration and the joy brought on by the arrival of his brother. I always invite my students to "find" themselves in this parable. As I look for myself in the parable, I must admit to being most like this elder brother. A friend of mine recently reminded me that there are more Pharisees per square inch in America today than at any time in the history of our land. Now, more than ever, we need to acknowledge our distance from our Father. We need to find ourselves, confess our own needs and return to be reconciled to him.

Yes, Jesus knows a great deal about sin! But sin does not dominate this parable. This is also a parable about mercy—mercy seen through love, joy and celebration. We see it most clearly in the characteristics of the father, especially if we place ourselves in the prodigal's sandals. For example, we find that we are loved so much by our father that we are allowed to leave home. The father's love is unconditional, but it is also unforced. The father allows for choice and, while there is much to say about bad choices, even those are allowed. The father provides both roots and wings.

We are watched as we leave, longed for until we return. And when we do, the father runs toward us with an embrace. That embrace smothers the confession of the prodigal with a hug, allowing grace to overwhelm the moment. The father's back is never turned on his son. And please know this to be a profound theological truth: the only child that God ever turned his back on was his own. This is one of the great acts of grace at Calvary, the rejection of an only son, so that such a rejection would never have to happen again.

The sin is forgiven. The lost are found. The dead are alive. More specifically, previous wrongs are set aside so we can rediscover who we were intended to be. In the process, the right to get even is surrendered. Remember Dietrich Bonhoeffer's words, "I consciously deny a rightful claim to justice." Mercy is applied so thick that one almost forgets what the sin was.

Everything changes. A ring is provided—the symbol of authority. Shoes are made available—the symbol of sonship. The finest robe is offered—the symbol of distinction. But then comes the banquet—a foretaste of the great messianic banquet we will experience in heaven, a community event and a communion feast of remembrance. The bread, the wine, the sacrifice and the mercy are all seen through this massive prompt of grace, which strangely allows for both a remembering and a forgetting at the same time. We come to the table remembering, but there is also a forgiveness and, in the mind of the father, a forgetting as well.

How can God possibly forget? This is mercy's highest reality, its most practical power. We can only speculate as to how our sins are not only forgiven but also forgotten. Let me tell you what I think: God can forget our sins so easily because he throws such memorable parties. At the very least, the party is so good that now the father remembers in a different way.

A MERCY THAT MATTERS

Simon Wiesenthal did not trivialize forgiveness. The father of the prodigal son did not cheapen grace. Both demonstrated that mercy can be costly. It can be painful. It might even appear to be destructive. But it is also liberating. Mercy frees the victim. As Jesus himself would demonstrate, forgiveness allows for a new story to begin, even while breaking the power of a remembered past. Forgiveness breaks the cycle of violence. In its place we find the assurance of pardon and our ability to pardon others. Maybe we don't forget, but as the prodigal son was given a memorable concluding banquet, we are allowed by grace and by choice to remember in a different way.

This kind of mercy—forgiving and forgetting, the mercy of the Christ of Calvary—is a challenge to our intellects and our human tendencies. Perhaps a metaphor might help. My mother had six children, and I always thought that was an act of supreme courage, the painful delivery of six babies. From time to time, as a young, inquisitive son, I would bring up this question of pain during the delivery process. Mom always had the same answer: "The pain of childbirth is always forgotten as soon as the new baby cries." It seemed to me that my mother consciously chose to forget the pain. There was a new life that came into the world, a new narrative, a new story, a replacement story for the pain, a story so wonderful that the old memories were transcended.

Consider also the Old Testament character Joseph. His brothers sell him into slavery. He spends a good part of his life in a foreign prison. In so many ways, his life is irreparably damaged, even destroyed. But when he finally connects with his brothers many years later, he makes this startling statement: "God has made me forget all of my trouble" (Genesis 41:51). For his ability to forget the old narrative, Joseph gives credit to the divine Initiator. From where else could this initiative come than from the One who has divine memory lapses? Joseph would go on to name one of his sons Manasseh, meaning "one who causes to be forgotten."

Where does all this take the Christian? Interestingly, to the Lord's table, a table of remembrance. We remember the broken body, the shed blood, the horrible crucifixion. That is the memory that points us to our Lord's mercy, his unconditional love, the great exchange of our sins for his righteousness, the blood covering for our sins and a new purity that allows us to have access to a holy God who remembers our sins no more.

The Eucharist liberates us from what would be a perpetual crisis of faith. Here we are allowed to reflect on the mercy of our Lord, a mercy of which we are now also capable.

6

GRACE
A Closer Look at Grace Applied

When it is a question of a sinner He does not merely stand still, open His arms and say: "Come hither." No, He stands there and waits, as the father of the lost son waited, rather He does not stand and wait, He goes forth to seek, as the shepherd sought the lost sheep, as the woman sought the lost coin. He goes—yet no, He has gone, but infinitely farther than any shepherd or any woman, He went, in sooth, the infinitely long way from being God to becoming man, and that way He went in search of sinners.

SØREN KIERKEGAARD

It is often difficult for us to understand, much less articulate, the tangible significance of grace. We feel so inadequate. It is not that we have not been recipients of grace; most of us would have a lifetime of examples, both human and divine, to talk about. But grace is such a precious reality, such a costly gift. As Christians, we talk about it constantly but can only begin to fathom its richness and fullness. Grace is overwhelming, yet easily assimilated. Tremendously costly, but freely given. Predictable, yet a total surprise. The world seems to be constantly in need of grace, yet, by definition, the supply is inexhaustible.

Reconciliation is the heart of the gospel, and mercy drives the process. It is grace, however, that elevates the process to a spiritual activity. I have already discussed grace as a prompt of the Spirit. It is certainly that.

When we see victims of injustice, hatred, immorality and downright evil rise above those circumstances and apply the balm of mercy to unlovable perpetrators, that kind of application has to be prompted by grace.

When grace is absent, our faith is diminished and our witness is unattractive. Without grace, at best we are pulled toward "a form of godliness, but [deny] its power" (2 Timothy 3:5). Our faith runs all the dangers of becoming institutionalized. "Whitewashed tombs" and dirty dishes—these are but two of many biblical metaphors for a life without grace (see Matthew 23:26-27). Without grace, we can only talk about a ministry—indeed, a ministry that has lost its joy, a ministry characterized by Levites and rabbis "pass[ing] by on the other side" (Luke 10:31-32). We may be students of the rules and have the ability to win every theological argument we encounter, but we also might be in grave danger of losing our most important relationships and perhaps inoculating many against the gospel we espouse.

On the other hand, the presence of grace makes our faith visible. The world is drawn to it like a magnet. Our gospel becomes real and irresistible, attractive to both the proud and the downtrodden. It is the absolute best we have to offer, and it costs us nothing. It cost God everything so that it could be freely offered to those who desperately need access to him.

Grace is part of the baton passing of reconciliation. Our Lord did it, and we have been left to continue the work. Again, grace is the defining characteristic of our walk with Jesus. "There is only one thing the world cannot do," says Gordon McDonald. "It cannot offer grace." But God can, and God has. As with love, we can show grace because he first showed grace to us—undeserved, unmerited, but the enabling light of our faith.

In the height of the war in Bosnia, I asked the Muslim imam from Sarajevo what I should be telling the American people. He surprised me with his answer: "Have the American Christians practice the best of their faith." He was referring to a faith demonstrably enhanced by grace. What God did for us and without us is now our best instinct and our highest value, what Mahatma Gandhi was missing when he said, "I'll become a Christian when Christians start acting more Christianly."

Finally, grace represents a definition of our faith that begins at the center, the center of a circle. Christ is the center of that circle and he is grace personified. Grace can temper the circumference, the litmus tests and theological hoops that determine for so many how the Christian life is lived. Jesus Christ is grace applied, a liberating grace that allows us to draw circles that include. Grace takes us to points of commonality. Grace allows us to build stronger human relationships as our faith becomes more attractive to the curious.

I feel the very best writing on grace is found in Philip Yancey's book *What's So Amazing About Grace?* This is a book of application, a book that should be read and reread yearly. Yancey helps us think about the real-world outworking and opportunities of grace in our lived experience. As for me, the characteristics of grace have been relevant at innumerable moments. Consider just three.

THE DAY OF GRACE IS NOT FOREVER

I went into the Marine Corps during a time of war. It was January 1966. The Vietnam War was moving along at full throttle, and we were ramping up to have more than 3.5 million Americans in uniform. I had not planned to be one of them. Military service never figured into my post-college career plans. But I happened to graduate when there was a war on, and it was my generation that was asked to fight. This would be new. This would certainly be exciting. The significance of this experience would be unique in my life, and I would learn a great deal about myself.

I would also make new friends and realize friendship that would last a lifetime. One new friend was Jim Fickler. We were friends for all the right reasons. We came from similar backgrounds, enjoyed similar pursuits and had similar short-term goals. The basis for our bond was a love of hunting and fishing. Jim came from Wisconsin, up by the Horicon Game Refuge, and had already shot more game and caught more fish at the tender age of twenty-five than most of us can imagine for a lifetime. If numbers are to be believed (and obviously one must allow for a certain stretching of statistics between friends, especially when it comes to hunting and fishing), Jim had already shot twenty-five deer and had caught thirty-eight muskellunge, a very large fish, one step removed (higher) in ferociousness and size from the northern pike.

Never having caught a single muskellunge in my life, I began this relationship with Jim with tremendous admiration. We trained together in the Grumman A-6A all-weather attack aircraft. We were both stationed at Cherry Point, North Carolina, in the same squadron and would be in the same squadron overseas as well. During our time in Vietnam, we both had bird dogs back in the States. Margaret Ann and I had a nice English setter that was being put through her paces at a game preserve in Iowa. Jim favored the Labrador retriever and had a black Lab being similarly trained in Wisconsin. We wanted to start a hunting preserve together, once we got back from Vietnam and out of the Marine Corps.

Jim and I were inseparable. Every chance we got, we would take an airplane to Cubi Point in the Philippines. Our concept of R & R was to shoot skeet on the naval base there. We would shoot boxes of shells for hours at a time, the barrels of our guns getting so hot we could hardly hold onto them.

Months went by. Our conversations continued. The dreams stayed intact. Each of us was to spend thirteen months in Vietnam and then "rotate" back to the States. Because I got there a couple of months earlier than Jim, I was the first to rotate home. A few weeks later, in early November 1968, my life was jolted by the worst news I could possibly imagine. After a night mission west of Danang, Jim's plane was missing.

"Missing." When you consider the triple-canopied jungles, the amount of real estate still uncharted, the mountainous regions of western Vietnam where he was flying, "missing" can appear to be a euphemism. But there was more to the news. Jim was not only missing, he was presumed to be dead. In the decades since, nothing has happened to change that presumption.

In the days and weeks after getting the news, I found myself going over every conversation Jim and I ever had: what we talked about, the thoughts we shared and the ever-present future that constantly needed to be rearticulated because it carried so much hope. As I continued to catalog our talks, I began to realize something more terrible than the death of a friend. In all the time I had known Jim, and in all the quality times we had together, I had not shared my faith with him. I had been a Christian all my life, yet my faith was not simply appropriated from my parents. Many times during my thirteen months in Vietnam, I had turned to this faith, simply because there was no place else to go.

My faith was real. But apparently it was not transferable. The news was good, at least for me, but now I had to wonder why it was not good enough to share with my friend Jim. I do not know what plans God had for Jim or how he might have revealed himself to him. All I know is that Jim did not hear it from me. For more years than I would like to remember, not a day would go by when I would not think of Jim, mourning not only his loss but also my inability to share an eternal reality with one who would experience, at least from my perspective, a premature death.

I have tried to rationalize. Maybe it was because we were young. We were flying into the jaws of death every night, and we still felt immortality was on our side. Somehow the vagaries and unfairness of war would pass us by. Death may have been all around us, but we were about to go home.

Now, of course, I know differently. We don't know how long we really have. What an obvious truth! How simplistically real. Jim was only twenty-five years old. He was not going to get one day older. And I kept my faith from him. I privatized the most precious gift I had ever received and, in Jim's case, ran out of time. The message is as clear as it is painful: the day of grace is not forever.

If the day of grace is not forever, there is an urgency to starting the process of reconciliation. But people need to be made ready for it, sides have to be prepared, and there is always a danger if we start too soon. I think of Bosnia and what the people in that troubled region saw and experienced. When World Vision first started our work there, we couldn't even use the word *reconciliation*. The environment was too raw. We could do more harm than good if we started prematurely.

On the other hand, the biblical admonition is not to let the sun go down on our wrath. Now, I don't think we have to solve every problem and reconcile every relationship before sunset. I do think, however, that this verse admonishes us to begin the process just as quickly as possible. Remember, we don't know how much time we have. The day of grace is not forever.

WHERE SIN INCREASES, GRACE INCREASES ALL THE MORE

During the time we have, however, grace cannot be exhausted. More grace exists than any amount of problems the world can dish out. No matter the hurts, the slights, the painful separations from loved ones, the intractability of global conflicts, we have a reservoir of grace that will never run dry.

I was standing on a bridge overlooking the Kagera River, the water boundary between Rwanda and Tanzania. It was early May 1994, less than a month since the genocide that rocked Rwanda had begun. The Interahamwe, marauding gangs of Hutus, were being encouraged to continue the killings; the graves of the Tutsis were only half full! At the same time, the Rwanda Patriotic Front was entering Rwanda from Uganda. These were Tutsis who had spent much of the last twenty years—since the last intertribal massacre—in Uganda. Their presence would ultimately put the Hutus to flight, stop the genocide and establish a different kind of rule for the country. But not until almost a million people would die!

The numbers are numbing, virtually impossible to fathom. It takes a long time to kill a million people, especially when the weapons of choice are clubs and knives. The Hutus did it with great intentionality, however, as teams of killers moved from village to village with lists in hand, sometimes with members of a village pointing the way, sometimes even with members of the church involved. The despised Tutsis were uncovered and met their fate without mercy.

There were mass graves, open pits and village wells—even churches—where bodies were discarded. But a good number were also thrown into the river and, as I stood on the bridge that day, I was allowed to see a sight that will haunt me until my death. Tens of thousands of bodies would ultimately flow down this river, and I saw enough of them that day to understand the depths of evil—and to have my own faith shaken to its core. Some of the bodies had been dead for days. Many were mutilated, showing again the savagery by which they had met their fate. Human dignity had disappeared. Sanctity of life meant nothing.

I stood transfixed on the bridge at Resumo Falls. To be candid, my faith was faltering. I found myself repeating the biblical definition of faith: "the substance of things hoped for, the evidence of things not seen" (Hebrews 11:1 KJV). "Where is the evidence?" I asked God. What was more real than what was passing before my eyes? I could see the destructiveness of sin, the manifestation of evil. What was more powerful than this? As I stood there, I did not have an answer.

God showed me two thing that day. As the bodies came over the falls, they were gathered by the back eddies of the swirling waters, arrested in time and space, moving continuously around in small groups, grotesquely and indecently held together by the force of the river. They did not simply float on down. They were being held in place for my extended observation. It was as if God was saying to me, "Look at this. This is not what I had ever intended. This is what happens when evil is allowed to get a foothold in the world. This is humanity's greatest inhumanity, and I don't want you to ever forget it!"

But a second thing happened as well. As the waters came over the falls, the force of the river hit the riverbed and a constant mist of water rose back up into the blue African sky. As the mist continued to rise, a rainbow spread from one side of the river to the other. Imagine that, a rainbow! A friend once told me that sometimes it takes a lot of rain before we get a rainbow. I had seen far too much that morning, and I desperately needed that rainbow.

For the Christian, the rainbow is both symbol and reality that we worship a promise-keeping God. On that day, it spoke to the constancy of God's love and grace. It reminded me again that he is still in control, no matter how chaotic the events. A security flooded over me, surprisingly. God became very real to me that day and his promises more sure. And one of those promises is simply this: "Where sin increased, grace increased all the more" (Romans 5:20).

What an amazing promise to cling to during the worst days of our lives and the worst crises in this world. No matter how great the difficulty, how horrific the sin, the Lord stands ready with an unlimited amount of grace—grace sufficient for the events of the day, even when evil appears to be in total control and command. A rainbow circumscribes our lives. It reminds us that grace has enough of its own capacity to win every time, each and every day, in every struggle encountered.

GRACE ELEVATES OUR HUMANITY

I do not like to travel during the Easter season. It is such a special time for me—the freshness of spring, the beauty of flowers, the Easter music and, of course, the underlying message itself. My faith is made whole at Easter time. All my memories of Easter are good and, if I had my druthers, I would always be worshiping in my home church at Easter.

But that was not to be the case this year. We arrived in Danang Province of central Vietnam a few days prior to Easter to work with the blind there. There were more than six thousand blind people in the province, and World Vision's task was to create income-generating opportunities for them so they would have the dignity of work and not be a drain on the fragile social infrastructure of the province.

The day was coming to an end. We were tired and ready to return to our hotel. One of our workers came up to me and mentioned a blind individual elsewhere in the city—a fifteen-year-old boy living in the slums. He had a beautiful voice, I was told, and liked to sing for visitors to the area. Would I be interested in seeing him?

There was very little to do besides sit in the hotel, so we agreed to go and meet this young man. When we got there, he was seated behind a table flanked by both Mom and Dad, and he wore one of those infectious smiles that seem to constantly radiate from Vietnamese youth. We found out that he was not only blind but also severely mentally disabled. That did nothing to dampen the smile, nor did it prevent him from beginning to share Vietnamese love songs with us. His parents continued to stand adoringly at his side.

It did not take us long to realize that he needed all the adoration he could get. Life had not come easily to him. As his story began to unfold, we began to feel that we were on holy ground.

In the last desperate days of the war in Vietnam, the North Vietnamese pushed through the province of Danang. The mother was having an affair with another man at the same time and became pregnant. By the time the child was born, she was so overcome with her guilt and shame that she tried to destroy the newborn. One night she left the house, hollowed out a shallow grave with her hands and attempted to bury her young son alive. But her husband had seen her. Horrified, he rushed to her and feverishly began to try to rescue the child. He did so, but not before the lack of oxygen had rendered the child blind and disabled.

He took the child and his wife back home. He gave the young boy his own name. He forgave his wife. As the boy grew up, this amazing gift of music was discovered. In this family's story, the echoes of another time, another son and another act of grace are clearly heard. Difficult times and enormous sins. Guilt that demands a sacrifice of innocence. A grave that could not hold the body. A father rescuing a son, forgiving the sinner, giving the son his own identity. And now that son was seated before us singing love songs. Easter music. The Easter song!

I am not sure I could have done what that husband did for his wife and child. It does make me see more clearly, however, what my heavenly Father did for me. The gift of his Son was not only an atonement for my sin, an exchange of his righteousness for my iniquity. The gift of his Son, as the supreme act of grace, elevates my humanity. The apostle was right: "I no longer live, but Christ lives in me" (Galatians 2:20). How did that happen? What allowed for this great exchange between sinful humanity and a holy God? Nothing less than a massive prompt of grace.

Grace can and will transform us. Grace makes us better people and improves our witness. Mercy is possible. Forgiving and forgetting the evil done against us is possible as well because we are now able to remember in a different way. This is the work of grace, and it is indeed amazing.

7

JUSTICE
Morality Cops and Biblical Justice

[Jerusalem's] princes . . . devour people, take treasures and precious things and make many widows. . . . Her officials . . . shed blood and kill people to make unjust gain. . . . The people of the land practice extortion and commit robbery; they oppress the poor and needy and mistreat the alien, denying them justice. "I looked for a man among them who would build up the wall and stand before me in the gap on behalf of the land so I would not have to destroy it, but I found none."

 EZEKIEL 22:25, 27, 29-30

W ho made you the international morality cop?" The question was meant to sting, to belittle. And with its asking, the tone was immediately set for the meeting. This was undoubtedly the most memorable question I was asked in my time at the State Department as the Ambassador-at-Large for International Religious Freedom. I was sitting in a supercharged atmosphere in an office in Beijing, China, across the table from the head of the Religious Affairs Bureau for China, Ye Xiawen. Surrounded by a substantial entourage, he was obviously relishing the situation. He had his "talking points" on a laptop in front of him and, each time I brought up issue after issue concerning the situation of religious freedom in China, an aide prompted him where to scroll for the much-rehearsed rebuttal.

I confess to not caring much for this man. Twenty years before, he had been a Red Guard working in Mao's regime. Now they had put him in a business suit, given him a laptop and pointed him to the right words as he did battle with a human rights nemesis from the West. In my mind, I saw a thug twenty years ago and an updated version of the same thug today.

But the question had to be answered. Was it legitimate for me to talk about a justice issue in communist China? As Ye Xiawen would point out, we had different histories, different cultures, different traditions and different systems. I found myself launching into a now familiar litany. I brought up all the international covenants that had been signed by China, starting with the Universal Declaration of Human Rights. I suggested that these covenants were more than clear when it came to the values we all espouse. Each of us had committed to certain principles, not the least of which was the principle of accountability inherent in all these international instruments. When something is amiss in one country, we have the right to draw attention to it.

"But we are not like you," Ye Xiawen countered. "We have a much different set of traditions." The implication, of course, was that he was more than pleased that China was not like us! I then began talking about what was "universal" in our understandings, what was essentially true for everyone regardless of historical backdrop. Frankly I should have known better. I had been part of a human rights dialogue with China the year before.

There were approximately thirty people in a room, an equal number from each country. Most were steeped in the legal profession. We talked for two straight days and made very little headway. At the end of this less-than-productive session, it finally struck me that we do indeed have very different starting points. We could not even agree on what the word *universal* meant. And if that was going to be a problem, it would be most difficult for us to come to a common understanding of principles upon which most human rights are based.

IS JUSTICE AN ABSOLUTE?

Might we ever get to a place where we are working with a universal and commonly shared meaning of what constitutes justice? Or is this important issue—an absolutely essential component of the reconciliation exercise—simply a function of culture, a subjective component fashioned in pluralism, imbedded in diversity, traditions and systems?

I have a very simple definition of justice: the proper use of power and authority to correct a wrong or satisfy a grievance. This begs immediate questions, of course: What is "proper"? What does "power and authority" mean? The first question is relatively easy to answer. The biblical text is rich in defining what a proper form of justice looks like. Perhaps Isaiah is most comprehensive:

> Is not this the kind of fasting I have chosen: to loose the chains of injustice and untie the chords of the yoke, to set the oppressed free and break every yoke? Is it not to share your food with the hungry and provide the poor wanderer with shelter—when you see the naked, to clothe him, and not to turn away from your own flesh and blood? (Isaiah 58:6-7)

Justice is the protection of human dignity, especially for those who have been marginalized by their circumstances. When it comes to widows and orphans, for example, the Bible gets very specific. Indeed, the alien, the fatherless and the widow dominate Scripture (for example, see Deuteronomy 24). It should also be noted, however, that the biblical text does not treat justice as a cognitive exercise but rather as something we *do*. It is always in the doing that we are fulfilling the biblical call to justice. Justice is active, a positive process of correcting wrongs.

We see justice as a transcendent issue, one that is very important to our Lord, an issue that speaks to one of the primary characteristics of our God and our ability to know him. That is, God is a just God. Consider this commentary on King Josiah: "'[Josiah] did what was right and just, so all went well with him. He defended the cause of the poor and needy, and so all went well. Is this not what it means to know me?' declares the LORD" (Jeremiah 22:15-16).

So why is justice being questioned in China? There are a couple of very simple answers. First, the worldview of a communist is anchored in atheism. Therefore the God who makes justice a transcendent issue is not known in Chinese thought. Second, in China, the state is much more important than the individual. The protection of human dignity is a distant second to the stability of the state; indeed, so distant that many times justice is not even taken seriously. What is "proper," then, will be seen differently in different parts of our world, and this is clearly the case in China.

But let's take a look at what might be a larger issue, that is, the "power and authority" mentioned in my definition of justice. Relatively speaking, and especially as we look at the rest of our world, we in the West have a great deal of both power and authority. For starters, we have access to knowledge. We have the tools to sort out the "knowledge explosion" that has taken place in our world. Our academic institutions and our technology, as well as the strength of our research libraries, give us unparalleled access to information. We know, and we know in real time.

Despite the economic uncertainties of the past few years, those in the West still experience far more financial stability and employment opportunities than most people around the world. And when our finances become destabilized, there are friends and institutions that will come to our aid. The safety nets are real. Help is never far away.

Relative to the rest of the world, we live a predictable existence. We have legitimate expectations for the present as well as the future. We have that wonderful ability to make realistic plans. Security is provided. Social services exist. There is much on which we can always count.

We have the ability to make decisions. What a gift! We decide whom to marry, how many children we will have and where we will send them to school. In general, we possess multiple options for virtually everything of importance to us. Granted, we are always susceptible to interruption, and sometimes those interruptions are painful. Catastrophic illnesses, natural disasters and premature deaths are not bound by economic and social status.

Consider, however, the other end of this power-and-authority continuum. In chapter two, I mentioned the terrible plight of a Chadian mother of twins. Her misfortune was to give birth during a famine, a famine that ultimately obliged her to choose which of her children would live. To me, this represents the very worst of poverty as well as a total lack of power or authority. This woman was forced to choose—a choice that precluded ethical considerations. However broad the continuum of power and authority might be, this young mother was definitely representing the most powerless. At the least, when we in the West examine our power and authority in the context of our culture, systems and traditions, we should feel the enormity of our responsibility. Jesus said, "From everyone who has been given much, much will be demanded" (Luke 12:48). Indeed there is greater accountability for what we do and how we implement this component of justice. Accountability is very much a part of the "doing" of justice.

Relative power and authority is also a function of identity. There are times in our lives when we seemingly have a great deal of power and authority. When I was president of World Vision, I was representing a financially strong organization working in more than one hundred countries around the world. When I traveled that world, I essentially had 350 million dollars in my pocket! This meant that we could command a great deal of attention. When we called meetings, people came. When we phoned individuals, the call would be returned. When we suggested partnering with other organizations, there would be immediate interest from those organizations.

The situation did not change when I arrived at the State Department. Now I was representing the United States, "the last superpower." I will never forget a line of thirteen black Mercedes, all showing the American flag, as our entourage was picked up in Tashkent, Uzbekistan. Specifically, I remember thinking, "I could get used to this!" Indeed many people do. This is the allure of power and authority. It can be seductive and have a very negative impact on those we are meant to serve.

What happens when these more worldly forms of power and authority are removed? This was a very real question for Margaret Ann and me when we began the Institute for Global Engagement. Our budget would be less than one million dollars annually, and a black Mercedes sporting the American flag would be nothing more than a distant memory. What happens when all these trappings are gone? This is a question for one's ego, but it is also a very deep theological and spiritual issue. Can a more humbled identity command justice? Gratefully there are a number of examples in our respective histories that suggest it can.

When Jesus was tempted by the devil, he refused these worldly trappings. The very Son of God "made himself nothing, taking the very nature of a servant. . . . He humbled himself and became obedient to death—even death on a cross!" (Philippians 2:7-8). And in so doing, he transformed the world. Mahatma Gandhi used passive resistance as his primary identifier, and thereby achieved great power and authority over those who could not counter this unusual "weapon." Martin Luther King Jr. employed nonviolence, a form of powerlessness that ultimately defeated those who would deny justice to others. Power and authority come from a credible witness, from trustworthy relationships, from proper motivation and from individuals who are demonstrably good.

There is a story told about a Japanese missionary named Kanaga. This man had a most unusual ministry. During World War II, he became a minister to American pilots who had parachuted out of airplanes that had been shot down by the Japanese. This was not a ministry that endeared him to other Japanese. The war was very brutal, to say the least, and any acts of kindness were not only random, they were frowned upon. Kanaga was seen as someone who was betraying his country, the war effort and the hopes of the Japanese people. Undeterred he continued to minister to the most vulnerable—and there was nothing more vulnerable than an American pilot who had fallen into the hands of the Japanese.

The ministry was both physically and emotionally hard on Kanaga. Over time, both his spirit and his physical abilities would be severely challenged. Some years after the war, Kanaga was invited to speak at Princeton University. As he made his way to the podium, it was obvious this was a man living in the last years of his life. He was prematurely old, bent and very frail. As he finished his address, one of the students in the audience turned to another and said, "He didn't have very much to say, did he?" At that, a woman turned around and said, "Son, when you are hanging on a cross, you don't have to say anything at all!"

Here we see an identity tied to a just God. Here we witness justice being properly pursued. Here we see real power and authority, a function of one who identifies with a God of all justice. The real question is always how we use our power and authority to support what is so near and dear to the heart of our Lord. We still have our orphans. We still have our widows. And yes, there continue to be those who have been beaten by robbers and left to die on the side of the road. How do we respond to the lost, the last and the least? How do we respond to those most vulnerable, those who have been marginalized? What would be our best methodologies for doing so? Both the powerful and the not-so-powerful have an obligation to perform.

It is this latter question that brings us back to the issue of justice. Is justice absolute, or is it simply a subjective function of the specific environments that we find within a very diverse world? Let me be very clear. I think that justice is absolute. Our knowledge of it might be limited and therefore relative, and our methodologies of implementation might vary, but there does exist an absolute standard for justice that is universal.

Would that we had an absolute knowledge of that biblical absolute. In our fallen world, as we look at that world "through a glass darkly," this is simply not the case. What we are left with is our own concept of what we think God meant by justice. In the words of Miroslav Volf, "We must therefore distinguish between our idea of God's justice and God's justice itself."[1] We should strive to know the mind of God, and as we get closer to him we will also get closer to what he has in mind for us when it comes to justice. The Bible is rich with references to justice; it is one of the dominating themes of Scripture. Reflecting on justice from a biblical perspective would produce a great deal of commonality for those who want to properly exercise power and authority.

The prophets were of one mind concerning justice, each providing a slightly different context. Hosea associates justice with a "return to your God" (Hosea 12:6). Amos suggests that we need to maintain justice in order to secure God's mercy (see Amos 5:15). Micah suggests that justice is one of three requirements: along with a love for mercy and humbly walking with God, we are to "act justly" (Micah 6:8).

However, differences of perspective will emerge at the point of implementation. And it is at this point that we do need to take into consideration the diversity that exists in our world—different traditions, cultures, histories, systems. Let me give you an example. Our work in the State Department on the issue of international religious freedom essentially involved two primary issues of discernment. First, what were the facts we encountered concerning religious freedom in a particular country? For the most part, information was readily available. We could visit the country. We could talk with the affected parties. We could discuss all of this with the appropriate government officials. We could secure additional reports from other sources, such as the nongovernmental organizations operating within that country. In general, the facts would emerge. They were discernable, and, for the most part, they were irrefutable.

A second level of discernment, however, was much more difficult. What do we do with what we now know? How do we implement a corrective to the problem we found? How do we handle what Volf calls "the problem of clashing justices"?[2] This was the thought behind my Chinese interlocutor's question, "Who made you the international morality cop?" And this is where we could use a little more humility and grace. The implementation of our methodology to correct an unjust situation very definitely needs an understanding of culture, traditions and individual systems.

I had to constantly remind myself when I was visiting foreign capitals, for example, that it took the United States 225 years to get to its present level of imperfection! We have reached a point of luxury where we can thoughtfully reflect on the issue of justice. But there are any number of countries in the world today still wrestling with extreme poverty, widespread illiteracy, periodic famine, messy border wars and the like. In Laos, for example, we desperately want greater attention given to the issue of religious freedom. With a 70-percent illiteracy rate and 40 percent of the population living below the poverty line, it is much more difficult for Laos to put religious freedom at the top of its agenda. For such countries, God's justice continues to be absolute; the process of change, however, must be cognizant of these very fragile environments. Implementing justice in a culture of vulnerability might very well be different from doing it in a developed nation.

Under the principles of the International Religious Freedom Act of 1998, we designated certain nations as "countries of particular concern," namely those who were violating what we felt to be universal standards of justice regarding this freedom. With some countries, we added sanctions to that designation, restricting trade with the United States, for example, or denying some other economic support. This implementation of justice, this exercise of power and authority, was hopefully done with a great deal of wisdom and discernment, as well as grace and humility, as the specific realities of a country were subjectively taken into account.

I think this is how we need to view justice. Our God has absolutized it. We do not dispute this fact. We must, however, take into account the limits to our own understanding in the methodologies we use to dispense justice in our world. Humility is always a helpful starting point. Grace always needs to be part of the application. Subjectivity is key.

MERCY POSES TOUGH QUESTIONS

As I have suggested, mercy deals with the past, providing forgiveness for the perpetrator's sin. Justice, on the other hand, begins to point to a preferred future and is inextricably tied to the component of peace. But there is also a relationship back to a remembered past, a past where mercy is essential. Mercy, practiced at its best, sometimes appears to play havoc with justice. For example, the father smothers the confession of the returning prodigal with a hug. A banquet follows. Where is justice? Jesus looks down from Calvary's cross and asks his Father to forgive those who had just driven the nails into his hands and feet. Not even a confession here! Where is justice? Dietrich Bonhoeffer appears to anticipate this question when he says that, when mercy and grace are allowed to have their day, he consciously surrenders his right to justice.

117

As we look backward to a sinful past, however forgiven, to what do we tie justice? Making justice only a legal concept does not seem to work. There are lots of things in this world that are legally right but morally wrong. We see politicians attaching their rationale for personal conduct to a "controlling legal authority." But this kind of legality simply "gets people off." Justice tied to morality, on the other hand, introduces a much higher standard of accountability.

Should we connect justice to relationships or to rules? If we revisit the parable of the prodigal son, this one is easily answered. The Pharisees and the elder brother were both rule oriented. The father cared more about relationships. He reminded the elder brother of a relationship reestablished, lost but found, dead but now alive. The relationship of a father to his son determined the implementation of justice.

Can cheap grace compromise justice? When I was in grade school, I took considerable delight in James Fenimore Cooper's *Leather Stocking Tales,* a series of stories from the frontier of eighteenth-century America. I devoured the books, vicariously living out the adventures. As an American literature major in college, I revisited those same novels, coming to a much different conclusion. I realized that these were books written in a context of total moral clarity without any ambiguity whatsoever. There were large categories of good and evil, and it was never difficult to tell the difference. The good guys walked upright; their blue eyes could see from horizon to horizon; they walked with a spring in their steps; their moccasins were soft and their weapons never misfired. The bad guys smelled like bear grease; they walked hunched over; their knives curled to sinister points; their faces were covered with scar tissue. Both good and evil lived in forests where it never rained too hard or snowed too long. Whenever there was an ambush planned to ensure a mighty victory of good over evil, some country bumpkin always managed to step on a dry twig (as Mark Twain humorously points out in his critique of

Cooper). The resounding crack alerted both sides to the presence of the other. The playing field was level and the battle proceeded to be fairly fought. At the end of the battle, evil slinked away.

The books are very pleasant reading and perhaps even make a good movie, but ultimately they depict an unreal world where everyone lives happily ever after. Most important, there is nothing at stake. There are no lasting consequences to bad deeds. No one is held accountable. What Cooper portrayed is an age of conflict without consequence. And yes, this kind of cheap grace compromises justice.

And then there is this thorny question related to justice: Does God love some people more than others? On the face of it, this might appear to be an absurd query. But look at the number of passages in Scripture that deal exclusively with the poor. There is simply no doubt that God shows some partiality toward the poor, if only to get our attention through the amount of Scripture that appears to be dedicated to them. Volf's insight is helpful here: "God treats people differently so that all are treated justly."[3]

This interesting thought can be underscored by one of Tony Campolo's stories. He tells about a boy from the inner city who became part of his outreach ministry. Part of that outreach was to take kids out of the city for a day in the country, supervised by adults who cared for them and wanted to provide a degree of freedom from the oppressiveness of the kids' normal environment. At the end of such a day, a staff member took this young boy back to his home. When they got there, the door was locked. They sat out on a street bench, keeping each other company, waiting for the boy's mother to come home.

Suppertime rolled around and there was still no mom. The staff member could see that the boy was growing hungry, so they got a pizza, which would meet at least the physical need of the young boy. The hours went by, it got dark and began to get cold, and still no mom.

Finally at about eleven o'clock that night, the boy saw his mother coming up the street, drunk out of her mind, with a man on each shoulder. "Mommy, Mommy," the boy cried and ran up to her. He tried to hug her, but she pushed him away. As the boy stood there, stunned, the mother hit him as hard as she could with a clenched fist. He fell to the ground, and she linked up again with her two male companions and staggered into the house.

Campolo finishes the story with this summary: "We always like to think that God loves everybody the same, but he doesn't. He loves some kids more than others because some, like this little boy, need to be loved more."

I agree. The "absolute" of justice has not changed. But to protect a boy made vulnerable by a horrendous environment, a massive amount of love needs to be made available. Grace is applied at the point of need, grace sufficient for this situation. Mercy and grace are always available in implementing justice. Indeed mercy and grace many times enable justice to be fully realized.

JUSTICE AND PEACE: AN EASIER LINKAGE

As I suggested earlier, both justice and peace work toward a preferred future, which is to say that both are forward looking. This is where the linkage between the two is most visible. Looking to that future, there is always a question when dealing with justice: How much is necessary? There are more than 100,000 Hutus still in jail in Rwanda, for example. How many Hutus have to be implicated in the genocide and convicted in a court of law in order to make sure justice is done? There are Serbs standing trial at The Hague for massive crimes against humanity. Is it enough simply to convict Milosevic? Must others be brought to justice as well? The simple answer is this: we need enough justice to ensure a lasting peace. We need enough justice, then, to make sure that hostilities do not break out again, that evil is not simply papered over, that deep wounds do not continue to fester. Peace, the product of the reconciliation process, is security for all. But peace is inextricably tied to justice. Justice without peace is often little more than revenge. Peace without justice is nothing more than an illusion. It cannot be sustained.

Justice remains an absolute that is fully known by a sovereign God and sought after by those of us who seek to know him better. But each hurt is different. No two conflicts are the same. National histories will vary as will the approach provided by national governments. A corporate entity might have less ability to demonstrate mercy. It may be easier for individuals to forgive. We arrive at the same point though our methods may vary from case to case. Those methodologies will always be subjective. Justice, however, remains an absolute.

THE ROLE OF JUSTICE IN RECONCILIATION

As we look at the four major components of reconciliation—truth telling, mercy, justice and peace—justice has a critical role to play. It is driven by the simple principle that sin has consequence. Justice makes sure that consequence is realized in the long term. We are held accountable for what we do. As such, justice gives predictability—and dignity— to the process. When done properly, justice will preclude both cheap forgiveness and shallow peace.

Justice makes sure that, at the end of the day, people get what they need. In some cases, people will get what they deserve. Justice is the healthy tension against the youthful exuberance of grace and mercy as it constantly remembers the responsibilities of all parties involved and holds each accountable.

Justice is ultimately made complete with peace: peace is the reward for justice. As such, justice becomes absolutely indispensable to reconciliation. It re-levels the playing field, not through blanket forgiveness, but by correcting a wrong or satisfying a grievance through the proper exercise of power and authority.

There is also a close relationship between justice and hope. One of the most important elements of a values-based society is an uncorrupted justice system. Without one, there is little hope for the future. Where there is corruption, when witnesses are brought in to lie, or juries are tampered with, or justices are bought off—or when truth is not allowed to be heard—this makes a mockery of a justice system. Indeed a corrupt justice system will lead a nation's populace to total despair. This kind of corruption defers hope and diminishes the possibility for security within a country. When justice is trivialized, reconciliation between peoples and between citizens and their government is impossible to accomplish.

In the past twenty-five years, I have been to more poor countries than rich ones. It never fails: the hope for development in a country is invariably linked to a mature justice system. The rule of law—predictable, transparent, understood by a nation's citizens, properly administered by those in power and authority—will provide untold hope for a nation that wants its tomorrows to be a little bit better than its today.

GRAND VISIONS AND SMALL STEPS

In his book *Exclusion and Embrace,* Miroslav Volf encourages us to think about the issue of justice in "grand visions and small steps."[4] The grand vision is nothing short of knowing the mind of God. Drawing ever closer to our Lord will bring us closer to this absolute of justice, in spite of our built-in shortcomings. Justice is such a key attribute of the Father. It is designed to protect human dignity and flows from the reality that each one of us has been created in the image of God. Admittedly these are grand visions. But they are also real visions, practically important and pragmatically valid. This is the basis for naming sin when we see it, correcting it when possible and making sure those who have been hurt by it are now helped. Growing closer to the God of history and the Christ of Calvary will always bring us closer to a proper manifestation of power and authority directed toward the peoples of the world.

But there are also small steps that each one of us can take. Many times these are the tangible implementations of structures that measure injustice, that remember (monitor and record), that create accountability, that promote our best instincts and our highest values and that ultimately hold parties accountable. I was involved with one such structure during my time in the State Department. In October 1998, both the Senate and the House passed the International Religious Freedom Act. The need for this piece of legislation was determined by an injustice that was being done throughout the world: the persecution of people because of their faith. More than 600 million people throughout the world (approximately 200 million of them Christian) were suffering the worst kinds of physical and mental abuse, primarily visited upon them by their own governments, because of how or what they believed. Global leadership was needed to place this issue on the front burners of our collective minds and to work toward change in what had become a horrific situation for people of faith. Both Houses unanimously approved the legislation, an indicator of how strongly Congress felt during a time when bipartisanism was rare.

The legislation was designed to hold countries accountable. It provided for an office in the State Department, led by an Ambassador-at-Large; I was its first occupant. The legislation also mandated a yearly report on religious freedom in 194 countries. This report would provide the occasion for House and Senate briefings on the issue of religious freedom as well. Finally, an independent commission was created to provide additional visibility for those who were suffering because of their faith. The issue had clearly gone public. We now had a process designed to ensure that all U.S. parties would be held accountable for the original intent of the legislation.

Of course, the legislation was not without its detractors. Would all of this public accountability hurt our diplomatic opportunities? Would the sanctions that were allowed under this legislation irreparably change our relationships with other countries? Were we *promoting* religious freedom or simply *punishing* countries where it did not exist and where punishment was not likely to make it materialize? Here were key questions because the answers would ultimately determine the kind of methodologies we would employ. Critics also asked hard questions about whether there is any clear international standard for determining religious freedom violations—a key justice issue and the one that was most forcefully brought to my attention during my visit to Beijing ("Who made you the international morality cop?"). Finally, there was a concern that this legislation might create a hierarchy of human rights, giving more attention to the issue of religious freedom than to other equally important freedoms.

All of these concerns are important. They continue to deserve reflection as this legislation is implemented. These concerns notwithstanding, ultimately no one in Congress had the nerve to vote against this act, regardless of the spoken cautions and the unspoken second-guessing that ensued. (In America, to vote against a bill labeled "religious freedom" is a little like voting a ban on apple pie.)

The written standards used for the International Religious Freedom Act came out of the international covenants that already existed, such as the Universal Declaration of Human Rights. Much of the same language regarding religious freedom was picked up in the International Covenant of Civil and Political Rights. The number of international agreements continues to mount. The language for international religious freedom, in general, is brought forward each time.

This language, so prevalent in the preamble to the U.S. legislation, had an additional positive aspect to it. Religious freedom is not a distinctively American idea. As former president Jimmy Carter liked to say, "America did not invent human rights. In many respects, human rights invented America." But this continues to be an issue that Americans feel strongly about. The International Religious Freedom Act allowed us to put our considerable shoulder to the already existing international wheel. It was this international language, based on international accords, that ultimately gave me an appropriate rationale for my China interlocutor, who was concerned about me becoming a morality cop.

The legislation also provided for a certain level of predictability. This took place as we implemented the act, and it speaks to the methodologies that we used. We personally called on every offending country that would allow us to visit. We were clear about the offense and specific about the reports we had received. We gave each country every opportunity to change. In some countries, we made multiple visits each year. In short, we gave diplomacy a chance and only used sanctions when our diplomatic avenues had been exhausted.

And we generated hope. As I discussed earlier, justice done properly brings about a genuine hope. I think this is the greatest byproduct of the legislation. Think of it: the last remaining superpower in the corridors of power is lifting up the persecuted of the world. American members of Congress are employing their power and authority to take the part of those being persecuted because of their faith. They are pleading their case, essentially lifting up their voices for those who have no voice. This is justice! Indeed, this is biblical justice.

All of this creates legitimate hope. People around the world who had fallen into despair because they had been made vulnerable to despotic governments now see an all-powerful country that is willing to take up their case.

In terms of religious freedom, this country has demonstrated an intent toward justice, a structure for justice and a methodology to implement that justice. In effect, we have a structural solution for a global problem. Because of this solution, we can help monitor and record acts of injustice, thereby remembering those who are suffering. We can be predictable, namely by speaking the truth without surprise. We have created accountability for victims and perpetrators by the information that we ourselves ultimately make public. In sum, we placed ourselves in the role of an international mediator (a nicer phrase than international morality cop!) by attempting to protect this all-important freedom through the very specific implementation of a justice-oriented structure. It is, in some ways, only one small step. But it does speak to our country's best instincts and highest values, and hopefully other countries will act similarly on their best instincts and values. More important and however unintended, it takes us a little bit closer to the mind of God.

COSTLY JUSTICE

Justice is the proper use of power and authority to correct a wrong or satisfy a grievance. In the exercise of that power and authority, sin is never trivialized. Indeed sin has consequences. Those consequences might be mitigated based on a specific situation. At its points of implementation, justice has a subjectivity to it that is a function of those situations.

But there is nothing cheap about justice. Our sins may have been forgiven and are remembered no more, but there were certainly consequences for those sins. In this regard, it is impossible to express in words God's decision to send his only Son into the world. The Word became flesh as God's pursuit of humanity became so intense that he allowed his Son to enter the world as a baby. Christ was born in a stable, with only the nightshift shepherds aware of what was happening, and his vulnerability would only increase as he became a political refugee in Egypt. Life was never easy, and we can only imagine the anguish of Gethsemane and the pain and humiliation of Calvary. Dying on a cross, outside the city, forsaken by disciples and his Father as well—here was the true alien.

Yes, here was consequence for sin. Justice was satisfied. The holiness of God could once again look upon humanity because humanity had been covered with a blood sacrifice, the blood of his own child. An exchange was made: our sin for his righteousness. God's need for justice was ultimately satisfied. We have been unbelievably blessed. But make no mistake about it: there was a consequence, there was a punishment, there was a body broken and much blood shed. Justice had its day, and it was anything but cheap!

Again, reconciliation is the heart of the gospel and mercy is the heart of reconciliation. Mercy and grace keep the full force of justice from being exercised. God's sense of justice was satisfied so acts of mercy could now be performed against this backdrop.

Certainly Adam and Eve experienced consequence for their sin; both were thrown out of the Garden. Cain experienced it as well; the consequence of murder was a life forever as a refugee. Noah lived through the destruction of the entire earth, a consequence of sin. In each case, however, mercy and grace tempered the demands of justice. For Adam and Eve, mercy came in the form of animal skins, a sacrifice and a shedding of blood for the wrong that had been done. Cain received a mark on his head, a mark that protected him in the midst of a world where life would never be the same. And Noah was given time to build an ark.

In each case, the consequence of sin did not destroy the relationship with a holy and righteous God. The Father knows much about the consequences of bad choices. Justice is done, but the relationship is never destroyed. The prodigal might have been humbled beyond words, but a party still awaited him. What a privilege we have, then, to be the ongoing expression of God's justice in his world!

8

PEACE

Security for All

If there is ever to be peace, it won't be authentic until each individual achieves peace within himself, expels all feelings of hatred for a race or group of people, or better, can dominate hatred and change it into something else, maybe even into love—or is that asking too much? It's the only solution.

ETTY HILLESUM, A YOUNG JEWISH MYSTIC
WHO DIED AT AUSCHWITZ

How wonderful it is to see a messenger coming across the mountains, bringing good news, the news of peace! He announces victory and says to Zion, "Your God is King!"

ISAIAH 52:7 (TEV)

I was slightly bemused by the individual sitting in front of me. An elderly man, a small man, probably somewhere in his early seventies—this was the individual the Vietnamese government "destined" me to see that morning. I was in Hanoi on a mission for the State Department, representing religious freedom. The Vietnamese had at that time (and unfortunately continue to have) a very spotty record when it comes to this freedom. On this day, however, the government was trying to put its best foot forward and had arranged for me to see an array of representatives from Vietnam's various faith communities.

Apparently they had a hard time finding a Protestant. It was never quite clear to me why this would be the case, because there are a small number of Protestant churches in and around Hanoi. But they had to go all the way to Haiphong, some forty miles to the east.

It was clear that the elderly man sitting in front of me was pleased to be there. He was all dressed up in an old brown suit, a wrinkled white shirt with a brown line along the top of the collar and a very wide tie. His smile went from ear to ear. As the government official who had arranged the meeting quietly left the room, I could sense the excitement building in my representative Protestant friend. He could not wait to talk to me.

He began the conversation by taking out a large bundle from his briefcase—in actuality an elaborate scarf that was protecting something very important to him. Slowly he began to peel back the corners of the scarf, being very careful not to bruise its contents and never losing that broad smile that seemed to dominate his face. Fold by fold, layer by layer, the scarf began to give up its contents as a mound of cloth was created around the site. Surely there was a pearl of great price somewhere in the center of this protective wrapping!

That pearl turned out to be a photograph, an old, yellowed, laminated photo of a group of young men standing in front of a building that could have been a church. My new friend excitedly told me that this was a picture taken in 1947 and it was of his Bible study class, taught by a young American missionary from the Christian and Missionary Alliance denomination. He was taller than the Vietnamese, obviously Western, and just as obviously respected and loved by this former member of that group, now sitting and talking excitedly before me.

The missionary in the picture was the first one to share the claims of Jesus Christ with this Vietnamese community. The Word was taught,

Christ was revealed and made real, and the peace that only God can give was experienced by a new group of Christian converts. More important, the worth of the gospel was made manifest in the presence of the young missionary. This was an incarnational presence: "The Word became flesh and made his dwelling among us" (John 1:14).

My new friend felt honored that someone would come ten thousand miles to share a message that would transform lives. Good news! A message of glad tidings, a message of peace. So precious that one would devote his entire life toward the opportunity to share it with a small group of Vietnamese. So precious that an elderly man's prized possession was a yellowed photograph that suggested friendships bound by divine intervention and sealed in a new covenant of peace. No wonder he was still excited. No wonder the smile continued to dominate his face. No wonder he continued to feel love for the foreigner who had entered his community in such a way that life would never be the same.

As I listened to him talk, feeling his excitement, indeed his joy—joy undimmed by the passing years—I could not help but remember that verse in Isaiah, "How beautiful . . . are the feet of those who bring good news" (Isaiah 52:7). How wonderful it is that there are people who have chosen to follow a heavenly call, expending their lives as messengers of glad tidings, people who are messengers of peace, of salvation, of the reign of God! When this peace takes hold, when the "reign of God" is felt within a person, when the God of history and the Christ of Calvary are finally embraced, we have the ultimate solution that endures—sometimes captured by a perpetual smile and a yellowed photograph.

But I was also struck by another stark reality. As previously defined in this book, peace is security for all. Further, to use the Hebrew word *shalom*, peace is God's intended wholeness and well-being for humanity. In this sense it is more than the absence of conflict; it is the way things are supposed to be. I found myself thinking about the life this man must have led since that day when he decided he would give his life to the Prince of Peace.

The history of Vietnam in the last fifty years is anything but peaceful. In fact, not long after this particular photograph had been taken the Vietnamese were locked in a long and bitter war with the French. Hundreds of thousands of Vietnamese would die. The Vietnamese people would be asked to absorb unspeakable hardships. In the course of that war, an entire social infrastructure would be lost. After the Vietnamese victory at Dien Bien Phu in 1953, they would sacrifice much to rebuild their country, to restore its infrastructure.

By the 1960s, reconstruction was complete. But now came a new war, and everything the Vietnamese had worked to restore was put at risk once again. In a conflict that would go on for almost a decade, virtually every bridge, power station, railroad marshalling yard, manufacturing plant and highway system would be destroyed. More than two million Vietnamese would lose their lives. Hundreds of thousands of them would be missing in action, forever lost to the country and the loved ones who managed to survive. Where was the peace in the life of this now elderly man who somehow made it through the last fifty years with a photograph intact?

Obviously the Prince of Peace transcends the difficulties of a war-torn country. The "peace of God, which transcends all understanding" (Philippians 4:7) has its own power and provides its own security. It is an eschatological reality carried in the present on the vehicle of hope. Various theologians have looked at the kingdom of God as a future reality breaking into the present, saying that our work for peace and justice is a matter of the kingdom coming and God's will being done here on earth as it already is in heaven. The tangible realities in the present, however—such as the memories of a young missionary's life lived incarnationally among friends a thousand miles from home—all legitimate a gospel whose future is anchored in peace. Hope present and accounted for! Hope made real in the life of a young messenger whose beautiful feet brought the news of both the kingdom that has come and the coming kingdom of our Lord, a kingdom that comes with the assurance of peace.

THE THINGS THAT MAKE FOR PEACE

I affirm the prophetic sense of peace that my photo-carrying Vietnamese friend made real for me that day. I am always in awe of what God has done already, completely without our help, yet biased totally in our favor. But there are also things that we can do. In addition to the prophetic power of peace there is also a process for peace, a process that relies heavily on the gift of common sense and the Golden Rule. How would we like to see our lives made more secure? And, much more importantly, how do we create security for ourselves in a way that maintains security for all? Martin Luther King Jr. said it best: "If one is not free, no one is free." The same can be said for this corporate process of peace: if one does not feel legitimately secure, no one else will feel secure. Peace will continue to be illusive. I'd like to suggest five steps in the process of peacemaking.

Respecting security. One of the first steps in peacemaking is to respect each other's need for security. The easiest way to do this is to respect common borders. Borders are important. They differentiate what is mine and what is yours. The key here is that they have to be protected on both sides. When the Cold War was coming to an end in the late 1980s, Mikhail Gorbachev, then leader of the Soviet Union, unilaterally initiated a move that suggests that he understood this principle of security on both sides of a border. He pulled back his troops from Eastern Europe, reducing the number of tanks there by about half. All the amphibious vehicles that would have been used to spearhead an attack across the waterways of Eastern Europe were also pulled back. Now, this was a major initiative. What Gorbachev was doing was respecting the importance of that border on both sides and creating a more secure environment for all by his unilateral action to reduce the weapons of war on his side. The West quickly saw the wisdom of such a move, applauded the step and reciprocated on its side of the border. A common border was affirmed and respected, and the exercise was universally applauded as one of the things that make for peace.

A border speaks to what we have in common and should never be used to isolate another country. When a country feels isolated, it will begin to act out its worst behavior. Look at what happened to Germany after World War I. Structurally and intentionally, that country was isolated because of the role it played in starting the First World War. In that isolation, however, the seeds of World War II were planted, paranoiac seeds ultimately sown in the heart of a dictator who would overcompensate for Germany's sense of isolation by beginning another war for world domination.

Or take a more recent example. For years we have been discussing and debating the impact of a missile shield that theoretically would create additional security for the free world. Much of the debate has centered around two themes. First, is the cost of the technology necessary to create the shield justified? Second, would it necessarily follow that successful security protection for our country means that other countries would feel more secure? If there is distrust among the nations, an airtight protection for one might raise legitimate fears in the minds of everyone else. If peace is security for all, a missile shield will have legitimate detractors, will raise legitimate concerns and probably will not create a lasting peace.

We always have to be careful when we isolate another country, especially when that isolation is built on a negative rationale. During my time in the State Department, the category of "rogue nation" was dropped in favor of the softer "country of particular concern." Frankly it was not an easy exercise to drop "rogue nation" from our diplomatic nomenclature. Historically this was the phrase we used to identify the pariah states (another descriptive, albeit unfortunate, phrase to describe countries). These were the words used to identify a few countries operating outside acceptable norms (sometimes norms established only by the West), countries illegally building up nuclear weapon reserves or other weapons of mass destruction, or countries that thumbed their noses at basic human rights.

The problem that arises is that countries so identified begin to feel isolated from the rest of the world. History has shown that the behavior of such countries is rarely changed for the good, but rather this isolation produces additional behavior that tends to be abhorrent to the rest of the world. The psychology inherent in such an exercise is simple and not unlike what takes place in a family when one member has been designated the black sheep. If the rest of the family thinks one child is indeed a black sheep, the child so designated will begin to act out with behavior to match the label.

Unfortunately the elimination of the designation "rogue nation" did not last long. The phrase is back in vogue. We now also have the "axis of evil" phrase, which once again does nothing more than isolate and exclude a country from the rest of the world, making it that much more difficult to have meaningful and productive dialogue with such a country. For reasons I frankly have difficulty fathoming, ours is a country that likes to publicly identify the offender in our midst.

As the ambassador for international religious freedom, my office was required to make a yearly report to Congress on the status of religious freedom in 194 countries. Putting that report together took literally thousands of man-hours and a production schedule that would frighten even the most addicted workaholic. But when it came time to present that voluminous report, invariably Congress—and the news media—really only wanted to know who the worst offenders were. "Who is on the list?" And, once a "list" of offenders was created, "Who was added to the list?" in subsequent years. This fascination with the list tended to trivialize much of our overall work and, unfortunately, isolated even further those countries that found themselves so designated. I continue to believe that such lists diminish the prospects for meaningful dialogue and add to the possibilities of excluding and isolating more countries in our world—none of which makes for peace.

As I write this, the affirmation of common borders between Israel and the Palestinians has all but been destroyed. Palestinians have violated the security of Israel through the use of suicide bombers while Israel has invaded and become an occupying force within much of the Palestinian territories. The "place and space" of the other has been violated. Now each feels isolated, alone and under threat. Ironically, in the history of Jewish war ethics, when a city was encircled, an escape route was always provided for those under siege. If an entire city were encircled, total annihilation was possible, an act that would destroy the Jewish sense of what a proper war ethic espoused. Additionally, if a city were totally isolated, the inhabitants inside would ultimately realize that they had nothing to lose and would put up a much fiercer struggle for their city.

This ethic at least acknowledges the problems with enemies that are isolated. Unfortunately the war of attrition that is presently going on in the Middle East would suggest that such thinking is no longer a consideration of those in charge. Therefore we have the Palestinians and Israelis, two people groups with a long, common history, now occupying essentially the same land, but each feeling the vulnerability of isolation. Their futures are inextricably linked, but there is too much wrong in the present to even notice. The violation of common borders continues to push peace aside.

Taking the first unilateral step. The second thing that makes for peace is the courage to take the first unilateral step to reduce the tension of the moment. Recall, for example, what President George W. Bush did when he first responded to the spy plane incident with China in the early part of his administration. The incident itself was most unfortunate. A Navy P-3 Orion, a slow-moving propeller plane chock full of electronic eavesdropping equipment, was flying its normal vigil just off the coast of China. Also, as was normal, Chinese MiGs were launched to harass the plane during its flight. The inevitable happened. A Chinese MiG and the American intelligence-gathering plane had a mid-air collision. On the heels of a most difficult period in China/America relations, which was punctuated by the inadvertent bombing of the Chinese Embassy in Belgrade, Chinese-American relationships were at an all-time low. The two countries were barely talking to one another. The Bush administration was brand-new, the antagonisms between the countries were quite old, and the worst possible thing that could happen was a military incident along the border.

The P-3 was sufficiently damaged so that it was forced to land on Hainan Island, part of China. The Chinese MiG broke up in flight and its pilot, one of the national heroes of present-day China, was lost. A search without recovery of his body only extenuated the tensions that were building between our two countries.

President Bush took the first step. He wrote a personal letter to the widow of the Chinese pilot. This was an extraordinary move, and it had the positive effect of reducing the tension between our two countries. In situations like this, it is very easy for invectives to be hurled back and forth with the result that a difficult situation in the present becomes even more difficult to solve in the future. That kind of cycle has to be broken. Trust has to be built. Each side has to feel some confidence that they can take a positive step of their own. When Bush wrote his letter to the grieving widow, he demonstrated the courage of preemptive action. He would go on to eventually issue an apology to the Chinese government for landing on their soil without permission. In the warp and woof of superpower interchanges, this may not seem to be much, but in the environment that existed at the time, it was enough for the Chinese to ratchet down their own rhetoric, allowing tensions to be diminished over time, and it ultimately led to the crew and aircraft being released back to America.

First steps are always important. And it takes courage, leadership and a touch of humility to launch that kind of preemptive, unilateral action. Without it, peace does not stand much of a chance.

Making an appropriate apology. In addition to preemptive action, a strategic appropriate apology will go a long way in creating peace. It is important to understand that an apology has to be appropriate. Just like cheap grace and cheap forgiveness, a cheap apology can bring more destruction than good. Some have called the 1990s in the United States an age of apology without accountability. In such an environment, apologies lose their meaning and, by extension, their value. Context is important, and so is timing. Understanding the facts and being accountable to their historical accuracy is indispensable when issuing an apology.

Let me give you a difficult example. I personally never felt obliged to apologize for my role in our war with Vietnam. I felt we were needed there, and I continue to feel that our efforts to keep the South from being dominated by the North were just, reasonable and an acceptable rationale for our participation in that conflict. At the same time, our presence there forced the 35 million people in South Vietnam to take sides. For the most part, they took our side. We were bringing in money. We were bringing in weapons. We were manning those weapons with the strongest military force the world had yet seen.

After a decision in the late 1960s that the war was not winnable, we left, fulfilling our own prediction of failure. Our allies in the South, our "friends" who had come to trust in our presence, were left alone, isolated by political realities in America and a new definition of "national interest."

As I said, I never felt any remorse about going. I do feel guilt, however, that we left early. Perhaps we should offer an apology to those who had much more to lose than any of us, and indeed, ultimately experienced that loss. It has been many years, and one might legitimately ask, "Why risk controversy with an unsolicited apology? Might we do more harm than good at this point?" I recognize the validity of these concerns. Maybe, however, we should also be concerned with those who spent years in "reeducation" camps. Maybe we should also demonstrate concern for those who no longer have the same educational opportunities or the same employment options that they once had. I have often thought that our angst over Vietnam was not primarily about winning or losing, but rather over the creation of victims, victims on all sides. Isn't it time for an apology, especially for those who struggle with a life wasted, hopes permanently dashed and a view of the future bordering on despair? Might we bring a measure of peace with such an apology? Sure it would be difficult. But that would make it more meaningful to those who lost so much. This too would begin to create trust, to rebuild relationships, to generate a different kind of foundation on which to re-create the potential for peace.

Admittedly an apology to our former allies in South Vietnam might be too difficult to do. But what about an apology to the people in Laos? We conducted a secret war there. I was part of that war, flying missions against the insurrection that was taking place in that country at the same time Vietnam was exploding. More bombs were dropped on Laos than on Germany during all of World War II, and today Laos suffers from the problem of unexploded ordnance. Cluster bombs still maim, and children continue to suffer from a war fought long ago. More than four hundred American planes were lost over Laos, an astounding figure. Today one of the most meaningful, trust-creating relationships that we have with the government of Laos is the crash site recovery and Missing in Action work we do jointly. Is it time to forge a more meaningful expression of our gratitude for Laotian help and a more substantive apology for a war that spilled over into the entire region of Southeast Asia? I think so.

Cambodia should not be left out of this exercise. We supported a government in Cambodia that could not continue after our departure from Southeast Asia. The Khmer Rouge took over, complete with a vengeance that ultimately destroyed a third of the population—as many as two million people. Do we not bear some responsibility for the "killing fields" of Cambodia? Are there other steps our country could take with Cambodia that would strengthen relationships, guard against distrust and paranoia, and forge the kind of positive bilateralism that is both predictable and, ultimately, peaceful? The courage of an "apology," in whatever form that might take, would be rewarded by a more peaceful Southeast Asia.

Glen Stassen, professor of ethics at Fuller Theological Seminary who has written widely on peacemaking, has this to say about the acknowledgment of wrongdoing: "Repentance does not lead nostalgically into the past but prophetically into the future." He goes on to say: "Unacknowledged guilt is not merely a moral sin but also, objectively seen, a powerful barrier to reconciliation. Therefore, honest acknowledgement is not a morally heroic option but an essential step for peacemaking."[1]

I should add that this is where the process of peace and the prophetic power of peace reinforce one another. An apology in the present is but another tangible sign of legitimate hope for the future. Stassen's words about repentance—and my own thoughts regarding apologies—tie back to truth telling. All of these elements of reconciliation do need to "kiss each other."

Speaking about the future together. The fourth thing that makes for peace is intentionally speaking about the future together. A discussion between antagonists about their hoped-for future eventually would uncover the aspirations that are common to both parties. Hark back to my argument with the commander of the Danang airbase. The base commander asked, "Do you have any children?" Yes, the common ground is our children's future, and it has to be discussed because our antagonism impacts all the generations that follow. Through his question, the base commander and I began to look to the future, a future not preoccupied by the war.

It is impossible to build a positive relationship with another person without discussing the future that will be common to both. This is why it was so disheartening when the human rights dialogue with China ended in the late 1990s. The United States no longer had an avenue to talk about human dignity and the sanctity of human life, though it is hard to find more important issues. For the Christian who believes that each one of us has been created in the image of God, the curtailment of a discussion of human dignity represents the ultimate failure of a relationship.

Thankfully, the dialogue that was stopped during my tenure at the State Department has now been renewed. Regular opportunities exist for American and Chinese diplomats to talk about this most sacred issue. This is the kind of dialogue that leads to the hoped-for future of *shalom*.

Acting as a third party. Finally, there are times when we approach the issue of peace as a third party. The conflict is between two other entities, but we have been asked to be a bridge—to be a go-between, an intermediary, a mediator, a reconciler, a conflict resolver. We are the catalyst, at least in the sense that we are there to facilitate change in a positive direction. We neither add nor detract from the change itself, but rather provide an environment within which positive change can take place.

A third-party role in facilitating peacemaking is similar to refereeing a basketball game. Good refs are not noticed. They are responsible for the application of certain rules, which in turn allow for the proper conduct in a given game. The two teams are the ones who bring the resources together that create a game. They are the ones who provide value—in this case, entertainment. The teams are certainly the ones with the most at stake. Referees are important, and a good, competitive basketball game cannot take place without them, but their sole duty is to put themselves in a position to make the best calls.

If peace is ever going to happen, if security is to become a reality, if all affected parties are ultimately going to feel secure, then the resources of peacemaking have to be provided by those with the most to gain. While studying conflict resolution in a master's program at George Mason University, our youngest son, Jesse, observed that the disputants in a conflict could actually become resources for its resolution:

> The number one rule of third party intervention consists of using those involved in a conflict as a resource and not a recipient of a service. This constitutes the very marrow of self-determination. Using disputants as a resource opens the door for them to take ownership of a desired outcome. If solutions are imposed by a third party without consulting those perpetuating and those affected by the conflict, peace becomes a mirage. Sustainable peace builds on systems that are already working and the people within those systems who desire peace. Sustainable peace anywhere depends primarily on local capabilities and the satisfaction of local needs. These needs are not met if people in conflict are being treated as recipients of a plan "that will work best for them."

A brief summary. Peace, the product of reconciliation, is never created in a vacuum. It is simply impossible to have peace in isolation from those around you. There is nothing unilateral about peace. The things that make for peace are not always easy. It will always be easier to isolate than to include. It is also easier to withdraw as opposed to having the courage to perform that preemptive first step. Apologies are never easy. Indeed the most difficult statement in the English language is "I am sorry." Finally, attempting to impose a solution from the outside is always easier but invariably less fruitful than watching the elements of peace slowly emerge from combatants who have been allowed the space to produce legitimate hopes for a much different future than the past would suggest.

Unfortunately the easy way is almost never the way of peace. Peacemaking is every bit as difficult as war making, and perhaps more so. The rewards of peacemaking, however, are uniformly positive: recipients are empowered. Positive resources are unleashed. Common futures are embraced. Relationships are reformulated based on trust, candor and predictable behavior. The playing field is leveled for everyone. Security is now the comfort zone for all.

But can there be more? Does this *process* for peace connect in ever-increasing tangible ways with *prophetic* peace, the peace of God, "which transcends all understanding" (Philippians 4:7)?

FINDING COMMON STORIES

One thing we know for sure: peace follows when all threats to peace have been removed. It is human to yearn for peace; this is a commonality that we have with one another. When people operate at their very best, they are drawn to one another, enduring relationships are established, conflict is minimized, and the vacuum of the human heart that yearns for peace has a legitimate chance of being properly filled.

But it takes intentionality to remove all threats to peace and create the possibility of prophetic peace. With that in mind, in the spring of 2002 we at the Institute for Global Engagement (IGE) invited a government delegation from Laos to visit the United States. These were the highest level of Lao government officials yet to visit and, in that sense, it was historic and significant. They were all members of the Lao National Front, the governmental entity responsible for interpreting the Laotian constitution. As such, the delegation was of those who ultimately decided on matters such as religious freedom, issues of ethnicity, and rights and responsibilities as their constitution is implemented.

Protocol requires that a government delegation be invited by a host government. With IGE's support, an invitation was extended from the office of Congressman Joseph Pitts of Pennsylvania. Pitts was a natural, given his long-standing interest in the issue of religious freedom. He is also a Christian.

Initially the Lao were reluctant to come. As I learned from a source later, the thought of a visit inspired fear. For starters, our countries have never been "close." Our history together, at least in the last twenty-five years, is tremendously conflicted. It includes the "secret war" previously mentioned, as well as the United States Commission on International Religious Freedom seeking to designate Laos as a "country of particular concern." Though no one from the commission had visited Laos, reports of violations of religious freedom were easy to come by, and sanctions on the country because of its abuse of religious liberty would have gone uncontested by a largely disinterested Congress.

Further, Laos is an extremely poor country with major endemic problems due to illiteracy, which conspires with poverty to keep it below the curve of healthy national development. As a poor country, over half of Laos's gross national product comes via global handouts. As mentioned before, Laos also found itself on the receiving end of a great deal of unexploded ordnance, the results of which continue to be visited upon those living in the large rural areas.

If ever there were two unequal entities on the global stage, it would be the United States and Laos. With this as a reality, why would Laotians want to come to the States and subject themselves to fifteen days of patronizing criticism?

And if this was not enough, there was also the potential criticism from hardliners in the Laotian government. At that time, the hardliners pretty much controlled the government, and there was a taint of betrayal on any Laotian accepting the hospitality of a country responsible for cluster bombs, napalm and Agent Orange.

Over many months we continued to push for the visit, volunteering to underwrite all the associated costs. Finally, just three weeks before the tentative dates for the visit, the Lao government gave a nod of approval and the delegation prepared itself to come. Parenthetically this favorable decision toward the visit would not have happened if I had not spent six visits over the preceding several years building relationships of trust and candor with Lao officials.

The delegation was led by Dr. Siho Bannavong, permanent vice president of the Lao National Front, governor of the Province of Vientiane and president of the Commission on Peace and Unity. His wife, Madam Kham, accompanied him. We also had the secretary of the cabinet for the Lao National Front, another vice president of the Front (who was Hmong and represented ethnic groups), the director of the Religious Affairs Bureau and the personal secretary of the president of the Lao National Front.

We jammed a lifetime of experiences into those fifteen days together, spending time at the State Department, the Justice Department and with personnel in USAID and the staff of the United States Commission on International Religious Freedom. The delegation met with a number of faith-based nongovernmental organizations already working inside Laos. We introduced them to the National Presbyterian Church of Washington, D.C., the National Cathedral and the largest Laotian Buddhist temple in the area.

Time was set aside to meet with Lao-Americans from every point of the political spectrum. Discussions were respectful, straightforward, intense—and immensely productive. We walked through most of the memorials on the Mall in D.C., including the Vietnam Memorial, and were hosted for lunch by the leaders of this country's POW/MIA effort. We carted the delegation off to Amish Country in Lancaster, Pennsylvania, where they saw an Amish farm in action and an Amish family living out their faith in freedom and security. I could almost feel God's hand at work as the Amish farmer explained how they meet in the basement of his home on Sunday to hold their church service. A religious minority, meeting in the "underground" house church, with all the protections of a sovereign nation—none of this went unnoticed by the Lao.

They were exposed to the orchestra at the Kennedy Center. We took them to New York City, to the United Nations, to a Broadway play and to Ground Zero. They were made graphically aware that even great countries are vulnerable without peace. Finally we took in a baseball game between the Baltimore Orioles and New York Yankees. Forty-six thousand people with absolutely no military presence in sight!

The visit was a highly significant event for all of us. We found we could talk about anything, laugh about everything. Candor was legitimated. Trust was now taken for granted. Socializing was acceptable, and Lao songs and American melodies were exchanged in those long hours spent together traveling from place to place.

As the time went on, we found ourselves telling more personal stories. As far as I'm concerned, stories are the highest form of communication. (Jesus spent much of his ministry telling stories.) You share stories with friends. Stories are personal, sometimes semi-private, heartfelt memories. Some stories are drawn out of a painful past but are allowed to be released among friends in the present. Intimate stories are told to friends with whom you feel secure, friends who make for peace.

During much of the visit, Madam Kham was the quiet member of the delegation. Laotian society has a tendency to be patriarchal, and certainly within the delegation it was hierarchal as well. As head of the delegation, her husband had to lead most of the discussions, and this was probably another reason why she had been reserved. But now we were in our last weekend together at a retreat center on Maryland's eastern shore. The meeting pressure of the last couple of weeks was behind us. The weekend was for relaxing. Everybody could be themselves, completely.

Perhaps the question to Madam Kham was inevitable: "How did you fare during the war?" How did someone "on the other side" of the conflict relate to the experiences of that time? We found that she had a story of her own—gripping, riveting and beautifully told.

It was 1968. The Sihos were already married but were separated by the war. Dr. Siho was an artillery officer in a unit some miles from their home. Time spent together was at a premium and, although they had already started their family, war kept the father busy with other things. Laos was going through the tragic experience of its own civil war.

There came a day when the "enemy" marched into Madam Kham's village and took her captive. She was accused of being a spy, of sharing secrets of war with her military husband. None of this was true, and she was doing nothing more for the war effort than trying to raise a one-year-old daughter while pregnant with their second child.

But in war, the absence of truth does not seem to hinder anyone. Her captors pronounced her guilty and prepared to execute her. She was tied up and taken to an opening in the forest, where a hole was dug at her feet. This was to be her grave. Decapitation would be the method of execution. As the digging progressed, the appointed executioner took practice swings with his sword, terrifying the young mother even as her child tried to figure out this new game.

Just as the hole was completed, the guards were distracted by shouts from the forest. A rifle shot rang out. A young man was brought out of the forest and immediately tied up. He too was accused of spying. But in wartime, a young man is a more valuable spoil of war than a pregnant woman, so the grave that was dug for Madam Kham was filled by the young captive. It was later discovered that an innocent man filled the grave meant for her: he had only gone to the woods to take care of personal hygiene needs. She was able to escape from her captors and return safely to her village.

Now, I had been a participant in the conflict that almost claimed Madam Kham's life. But I could not begin to relate to what a mother must go through, having her children alone, forever wondering about the safety of her husband, fighting the despair that comes with the proximity of death. No, I was not the best one to relate to that story. But my wife, Margaret Ann, was. She began to share her own experiences during that time and, as she did, Madam Kham nodded understandingly. Women know how to connect. Motherhood increases that connection.

Margaret Ann was also pregnant while I was in Vietnam, fighting a war in which we were all participants. Relative to Madam Kham, Margaret Ann was safe but terrified that she would not see her husband again. For the two women, 1968 would be a most memorable year, and one they hoped never to have to repeat. Each one seemed to know the feelings of the other: how a heart aches when a loved one is not close; concerns for children who may not see their father again; the fear and insecurity of potentially going through life alone. I have often felt that if mothers could vote on war, there would never be another one.

I sat there and listened to two women tell their stories—so many things in common, so many things that were different. A Laotian mother fighting for her life. An American mother praying for the normalcy that war had put on hold. Conversation flowed out of a strong bond of commonality. A friendship had been secured. The relationships were far enough along that each knew that this new place was a safe place. Stories could be shared because the deeper meanings of those stories had also been shared. They were stories of life and death, of struggle and sacrifice, of doubts and fears, of hopes matched by a desire that the hopes could be made real. These stories crossed the divides of culture, transcended the events of history and brought the representatives of nations once hostile to one another to a place of deep respect and understanding.

I am often amazed how God brings people into our lives who seem to bring closure to something begun many years before. A simple question, "How did you fare during the war?" brings a new reality and an enduring relationship to people who have known each other for less than fifteen days. This is the awesomeness of God at work! These are the things that make for peace.

Later that day, I made it a point to reconnect with Madam Kham. I told her how much I appreciated her story. I also suggested that she had experienced something that represented one of the core principles of the Christian faith. An innocent man filled a grave that should have been mine. An innocent person was executed so that I might go free. I asked Madam Kham if she grasped the principle that had been lived out by our Lord and Savior, Jesus Christ, the One who gave his life as a divine substitution for our own sins. She allowed that she did, and went on to say that that day had brought her closer to her God than she had ever been before.

I don't know the direction God will take Madam Kham's life. I do know that seeds were planted, seeds were watered. Our God, in his infinite grace and mercy, will hold himself solely responsible for the increase. I do know that three stories were told that day, two by women who had much in common and one suggesting the greatest commonality of all: a God of all. I also know that there was no longer any fear on the part of the delegation. A tentative trust had given way to an enduring peace, a peace that was understood, individually felt, personally experienced, seen in others and undergirded by a divine act of mercy.

For peace to work, justice has to be satisfied. Our Lord, absorbing the executioners' blows and occupying an early grave, satisfied the need for justice on the part of a holy and righteous God. Because of that preemptive action, peace is more than a possibility. Relationships that are allowed to flourish in the context of peace are just as real and just as possible as the suffering we experience along the way. For the Christian, this is merely a foretaste. Conflicts will cease but peace will endure until that time when the Prince of Peace will return like the messenger who runs over the mountain (see Isaiah 52:7).

For now, we are privileged and blessed to see relationships that evolve to the point where trust and safety allow us to share our most intimate memories, connecting our stories with his story. Today we see life through a yellowed photograph of when we first heard the news that forever captured our interest. Someday the image will be replaced by a face-to-face appointment with the God of history. The Prince of Peace will announce the time. And we will say again, "How beautiful . . . are the feet of those who bring good news, who proclaim peace, who bring good tidings, who proclaim salvation" (Isaiah 52:7).

WHAT WE DO

9

EFFECTIVENESS
Extending the Hands

One thing which has thus far escaped globalization is our collective ability to act globally. Since our mutual dependence is already by and large global, our moral responsibility for each other is real as never before. Given, however, the economic bias of globalization, taking responsibility becomes yet more difficult. Our sensitivity is assaulted by sights, which are bound to trigger our moral impulse to help—yet it is far from obvious what we could do to bring relief and succour to the sufferers.

ZYGMUNT BAUMAN

When I became president of World Vision in 1987, my installation charge came from the parable of the good Samaritan. I was charged to go out and find people of passion and compassion, enlisting the aid of good Samaritans everywhere. I also was charged to identify those who know and love their neighbor, who are being called to embrace a world of change and challenge.

But the more interesting part of my charge was that, when I was unable to find any more good Samaritans, I was to go out and make them. Specifically to make them out of "Levites"—those good-hearted souls whose church calendars are so full they end up neglecting both the larger family of God and immediate family members. I was also given the task of making them out of "rabbis"—those products of and contributors to institutionalized religion, most of it man-made, who have lost their joy in the ministry itself.

Not only that, I was further charged to make them out of "innkeepers"—members of corporate America who have the resources to help but who need to know how and why to invest, and that their investment will make a difference. Finally I was charged to make good Samaritans out of "robbers"—those who would steal our hopes, our dreams and our dignity, who would steal the very opportunity to demonstrate our ability to be good neighbors. Leaders who put self higher than those they have called to serve, politicians whose only guidepost is the latest poll, business leaders who put profits ahead of persons—robbers, every one.

In the course of the next fifteen years, I realized that there was an even larger problem than simply finding, or even making, people of compassion. There is a potentially huge stumbling block inherent in the exercise of global engagement that can prove to be downright paralyzing to those who are making their way out on that proverbial dance floor. Simply put, our Jericho Road is a whole lot wider and longer, not to mention more complicated, than the one traveled by the good Samaritan. To call the obvious into focus, there is certainly more than a single victim on our road today. Our Jericho Road is as wide as the information highway. Our victims are as numerous as the bandwidth we can afford. On a good day, we are humbled by the amount of hurt that exists in the twenty-first century. On a bad day, we are paralyzed by the overwhelming needs.

Putting all of this in the context of globalization, Zygmunt Bauman, professor emeritus at Leeds University, England, surmises that "this is, arguably, where the moral problem of our globalizing world is rooted— in that abysmal gap between the suffering we see and our ability to help the sufferers." He goes on to suggest that this is a problem that our ancestors never faced: "Their moral responsibility and their capacity to act matched each other."[1] But our access is so good, our information so valid, our technological vehicles that transmit into our households and our consciousness on a daily basis so credible that we have the unavoidable situation of being sure of today's specific needs in distant parts of our world without the individual capacities to do much about it. Relative to the challenges today, the good Samaritan had it easy! In Bauman's words, "The challenges to our moral conscience exceed many times over that conscience's ability to cope and stand up to the challenge. To restore the lost world balance, we would need 'artificial hands' stretching as far as our artificial eyes are able to."[2]

We are not without some helpful models as we try to sort out what can be a major ethical dilemma. We have the insightful simplicity of Mother Teresa's response to a series of cynical questions: "How can you attempt to wipe out poverty in Calcutta? Everyone you touch appears to be near death, or dies. How can you ever hope to be successful?" To all of this, Mother Teresa replies, "God has not called me to be successful, only obedient." In that practical, commonsensical response, she has given us words, concepts and a theological base that is tremendously liberating in a world of overwhelming need. We are called to be faithful. We are called to be obedient. We plant and we water. Success belongs to God; he brings the increase. This means that the scorekeeping is his as well. We do what we can do; we let God do the rest. In a world where it often looks like the bad guys are winning, it is tremendously liberating to allow God to keep score.

We worry a great deal about the fact that our work is never really done. In this we fail to remember that Jesus did not heal everyone. He did not feed everyone. He did not restore everyone to physical and emotional wholeness. And he certainly did not resurrect everyone. Why in the world would we feel that we have to perform at a better rate? He was obedient, however, and ultimately that was the measure of his incarnational witness to the peoples of this earth. We need to be obedient.

At the same time, it is only common sense to find the best organizations and the best programs with which to affiliate as we take on the practical exercise of global engagement. This is how we begin to build those "artificial hands" that bring comfort in a world of hurt. Certainly not all organizations are the same. Some are very much better than others at engaging this world. Some have a mindset and a proven methodology for collaboration, which is absolutely essential in a world where no one has all the answers, all the resources or all the solutions to problems. There are ways to fashion positive synergies, legitimate partnerships where one plus one equals at least three, and hopefully better. Some are open to change, receptive to individual leadership and ready for new ideas brought from outside the organization.

We are grateful for Mother Teresa's theology and practical good sense. She certainly had a theology that touched the ground, especially in the most difficult settings of our world. But we also need practical good sense as we begin to assess the human resources that are available to us as we engage this world. Simply put, we need to find and associate with those organizations, programs, philosophies and people that collectively give us the best chance of avoiding paralysis, maintaining our faithfulness and being good neighbors to those the Lord puts on our hearts and in our paths. That is what this chapter is about.

A CAPACITY FOR RENEWAL

At this point, you may be wondering what you can do to make a difference. Following up on the ingredients for effective reconciliation that we developed in the central part of this book, there are things you will need to know to contribute to global engagement and reconciliation.

Most of you will be looking for organizations that seek to be relevant in today's difficult world. As you look to make the best choice of such an organization, there are two overriding characteristics that need to be identified: ability to reform and ability to partner.

An ability to reform. First, what is the potential and inclination within the organization toward change? The world is indeed changing at exponential rates, and the static performer will be quickly dismissed. This principle applies both to individuals and to the organizations they represent. The redeemed community needs to be *continually* redeemed.

Earlier I commented on the tragedy that unfolded in Rwanda. By late summer, in addition to more than 800,000 people killed through genocide, refugees of that conflict were dying at the rate of 10,000 a day in the camps along the border. That is a number that can boggle the mind. Indeed it can be paralyzing for both an organization and an individual.

I can remember calling a World Vision staff member who was working in one of those camps. It was August 1994. In the course of the conversation, I asked him what sustained him, what gave him hope in the midst of such a tragedy. His answer surprised me and horrified me at the same time. "Today was a good day," he said. "Today we got all the bodies buried. Now the children don't have to walk past that huge pile of bodies when they come into the dispensary for their health needs."

This global engagement was not for the fainthearted! We had to rotate staff in and out of refugee camps like this at least once every four weeks. The psychological and emotional toll was just too great. People had to be renewed.

John Schenk was a photojournalist working with World Vision in Rwanda at the time of the genocide. He had more than ten years of experience in Africa and had covered some of the most chaotic human dramas in the history of the world. Slowly but surely, the sights, the smells, the pain and the suffering were all taking a toll on John. One day, early in the genocide, he was filming the massacre site at the church in Nyamata. More than six thousand Rwandans had died there after fleeing to the church in hopes of finding sanctuary.

The new government in Rwanda decided to leave the bodies exactly where they fell to provide a monument to the unspeakable, an example of what had happened in all too many places throughout that war-torn country. As John looked at the bodies of dead men and women, boys and girls, saw the suffering that had ensued, the torture that was part of this particular corner of the killing field, he tried to focus in a detached way through the lens of his camera. But there was a voice in his head and it would not go away. He found himself saying over and over again, "God, can I go home now?"

"God, can I go home now?" Sometimes we see too much. Sometimes we stay too long. If the time for renewal is put off too long, an individual can be destroyed. Change is necessary. Reform is good. An organization that is sensitive to the needs of its individuals in this regard is a good organization for which to work. These are the organizations that value people. These are the organizations that are mature enough to assimilate this kind of necessary change.

Institutions also need to change. Look at the military in the United States from the war in Vietnam to today. Vietnam was a very difficult place to fight a war. Additionally the political side to this conflict ultimately determined what the military could do, essentially diminishing the potential for victory. There were frustrations as the war evolved. There were mistakes. There were enough bad examples all around for all of us to learn something.

The military picked up a very negative taint during that time. The criticism was not always fair and the finger pointing was not always appropriate. After Vietnam, however, came a great deal of reflection within the ranks of the senior officers of the U.S. military. From Vietnam onward, reform took place. When it came time to fight the Gulf War in the early 1990s, that reform was complete, and by then it was a different military. The strategies were different, the methodologies employed were different, what the media was allowed to report was certainly different, and the outcome was much different as well. In fact, the only thing Vietnam had in common with the Gulf War was that American troops participated in both.

The military saw a need to reform. Critical thinking about how war should be fought eventuated in an all-volunteer military that put a premium on education concerning new geopolitical realities. By the end of the Gulf War, the military was one of the most respected institutions in the United States. In this respect, political institutions could learn a lot from the military. As I write this, campaign finance reform has just had some initial success in Congress, but it remains to be seen whether or not the necessary changes—reforms that would generate renewed respect for our political process—will happen.

The media is another institution in our country that absolutely must go through a reformation process. There appears to be considerable professional flailing around on a continuum between good solid journalism and so-so entertainment. Good journalism is being diminished by soft news. The media would do well to look at the U.S. military for a methodology of reformation.

Change forces us to look at our organizations and institutions through lenses that are adjusted to new realities. In terms of global engagement, our reality has undergone dramatic changes in the past several years. The growth of complex humanitarian emergencies (disasters that impact an entire country or region of the world), the advent of identity wars (many of which are fought along religious lines), the widespread use of terror, the emergence of the suicide bomber—these demonstrate unequivocally that our world has changed. For an organization to be relevant and for individuals to be relevant within that organization, renewal and reform have to be part of the corporate culture.

An ability to partner. The second key characteristic of a relevant organization in the twenty-first century is the ability to collaborate. There is simply too much need in the world; no one organization can make a dent by itself. No organization has all the tools or the resources to be effective in going it alone. The twenty-first century will demonstrate—and I am absolutely confident on this point—that organizations that know how to form strategic alliances, to collaborate with others for as long as that collaboration might be needed, will have the largest impact. These organizations will have the greatest extension of those "artificial hands" that Bauman talks about.

Collaboration is not easy. It might be the most exhausting exercise an organization ever attempts. The human tendency is to seek to remain free from someone else's entanglements, to go it alone, to "stick to one's own knitting." That tendency, however, may ultimately deprive the organization of its maximum impact.

Collaboration should only be entered into when the *whole* of the effort is greater than the *sum* of its collective parts. If one plus one only equals two, it is not worth it. A simple example: one organization has the ability to drill for and find clean water. Another has the ability to put in place a medical infrastructure at the community level. Can you imagine what the presence of pure water and good medical care can do to the long-term viability of a rural community? Good medical practice without that pure water will always fall short of a sustainable solution to a community's need. On the other hand, clean water without a concomitant medical infrastructure will only take care of part of the problem. Sustainable development, in our best understanding of what that means, now has a legitimate chance in such a community. Clearly, if this is possible through organizational collaboration, that kind of partnership should be strongly encouraged.

Obviously collaborations take place on more than merely programmatic levels. This is where the exercise gets trickier. For a collaboration to succeed, there has to be a coherence of culture, namely enough similarity in the ethos of each organization that will allow them to work well together. For example, World Vision did its development work through the community. World Relief, on the other hand, worked through the local church. The theological underpinnings of both organizations were the same, however, and this cultural coherence has made it relatively easy for the two organizations to partner around the world. Similarly Catholic Relief and Mercy Corps operate from the same Catholic underpinnings, allowing for easy collaborations between the two.

Congruency of mission is another consideration. Organizations need to keep their individual missions intact as they work together with other groups. If a collaboration is going to cause an organization to lose its focus, one would need to think long and hard before entering into such an alliance.

There also needs to be a commitment to similar values. Most organizations have a hierarchy of values from which they choose not to deviate. If a collaboration is going to risk changing the values of one of the individual entities, the collaboration is destined to fail. Values give an organization its identity. Many times, values are responsible for motivation as well as focus. In sum, the general rule is this: a collaboration is good if there is a congruency of mission, a coherency of culture and a commitment to values such that the identity of either entity is not compromised. Stay away from anything that does not fit this description.

All of this suggests that discernment is extremely important in choosing partners. An organization that effectively selects partners is usually one that is reflective, takes its time, counts the cost and attempts to measure the collective impact in any partnership arrangement.

One final word on collaborations: to be successful, the collaboration has to take place at all levels within an organization. I have found it fairly easy for CEOs to agree on a particular way forward. But it has also been my experience that other members of the organization may have considerably more trouble, especially those who have individual goals created prior to the new alliance. For example, fundraisers have a hard time with collaborations. Interestingly, but not unpredictably, many collaborations fail at the point of fundraising. "Who will fund the partnership? My donors or your donors? Will we share the donors?" Collaborations also fail at points of credit. Who is going to get the credit if this enterprise succeeds or, more importantly, who takes the fall if things don't go well?

MAKING THE CASE FOR NONGOVERNMENTAL ORGANIZATIONS

We may wonder what we as individuals can do about anything—but that is why we need to partner with like-minded people in either government, nongovernmental (NGO) or multilateral (for example, the United Nations) organizations. Although a great deal can be said about individual accomplishments, inevitably those accomplishments need to be attached to an infrastructure larger than the individual if relevance and impact are going to be achieved.

It will become immediately obvious that I am partial to the so-called "non-state actors," those other-than-government bodies (NGOs) that play a role in international affairs. I have worked with both: eleven years as president of World Vision, a large and credible NGO active in more than one hundred countries, and two years within the United States State Department. Each has a role to play in international affairs. Each has its share of dedicated employees focused on the exercise at hand. Each has an essential mission and works fairly effectively and purposely toward meeting the goals of that mission. But the NGO world provides much greater opportunities to steward the resources available and maximize energies expended.

By definition, government work is always biased by politics. Irritatingly for the purist, there is a thick overlay of political reality on virtually every major decision that is made by government entities. The fine art of compromise is a necessity if one values a career in government. Expectations have to be managed, and this normally ends up taking you to a lower common denominator. Great expectations and high hopes tend to be ratcheted down with the daily grind of governmental realities, eventuating in rather trivial accomplishments for all the energy expended.

More specifically, I found it very difficult in government to take a long view. It always seemed that the critical timing mechanism was tied to the first Tuesday in November and what the balance of power would look like after the next election. Because sustainable solutions are almost always long-term, this short time frame created a myopic perspective and, many times, produced nothing more than knee-jerk reactions.

I was also struck by the emphasis on symptoms rather than causes. In the Office of International Religious Freedom, a symptomatic approach would unfold in the following manner. When we got someone out of a foreign jail, normally a release from despotic, authoritarian forces that cared little about human rights, there was always great rejoicing. But rarely did anyone raise the question of why people went to jail in the first place. It is long-term sustainable solutions that get at the cause of a particular problem. Governmental culture is not the most conducive for solutions that endure.

Finally, all governmental work is bureaucratic to some degree. Bureaucracy can mean many things, but for me it came to mean a lack of flexibility, of organizational nimbleness and of rapid response. There were always layers of interested bureaucrats who would ask one more question, demand one more opinion, caution against one more remote possibility that existed, in my mind, only in theory. Granted, people who know me realize that I am not "wired" for government work, but the limitations in a governmental approach need to be very carefully considered by anyone who is thinking about extending hands around the world through the vehicle of government agencies.

The NGO world, on the other hand, has the ability to move quickly, concentrate on the long haul, focus on the causes of endemic problems and create the kind of sustainability that permanently solves problems. This is not to say that the NGO world always proceeds this way; it is simply to note that an NGO approach is much easier to implement, with much greater possibilities of success than the more constrained approach one would find in government.

Some years ago, Jessica Mathews, now president of the Carnegie Endowment for International Peace, wrote an article in *Foreign Affairs* called "Power Shift." She makes an excellent case for non-state actors (nonambassadors, nonpresidents, non-State Department types) moving across semipermeable borders, generating effective humanitarian assistance that is other than what might flow from government entities. Speaking about the current relevance of NGOs, she says:

> Today NGOs deliver more official development assistance than the entire U.N. system (excluding the World Bank and the International Monetary Fund). In many countries they are delivering the services—in urban and rural community development, education, and healthcare—that faltering governments can no longer manage.

Mathews goes on to suggest that this current relevance is only going to be enhanced in the years to come: "Non-state actors have never before approached their current strength. And a still larger role likely lies ahead." Drawing the comparison between the NGO community and national governments, she concludes with this strong statement:

> Internationally, in both the poorest and richest countries, NGOs, when adequately funded, can out perform government in the deliv-

ery of many public services. Their growth, along with that of the other elements of civil society, can strengthen the fabric of the many still fragile democracies. And they are better than governments at dealing with problems that grow slowly and affect society through their cumulative effect on individuals—the "soft" threats of environmental degradation, denial of human rights, population growth, poverty, and lack of development that may already be causing more deaths and conflict than our traditional acts of aggression.[3]

But negative comparisons are only useful to a point. Again, both government and NGO sources are necessary if we are to begin to make progress on the problems in today's world. It is far more useful to see how these various entities work together, each contributing its best expertise and, in combination, forging effective solutions.

John Paul Lederach, one of today's most gifted practitioners and proponents of reconciliation, gives us another lens with which to view effective engagement. He sketches out a triangle, the base of which is occupied by the indigenous population, the local church, community and village governance—essentially the mass of people who, in difficult circumstances, are experiencing the most suffering. This broad-based bottom—stretched along the cruel corners of our world—is characterized by suffering without resource, information without response and passions without power.

At the top of this triangle you find the diplomatic elite, those who have achieved power based on politics. Richard Holbrook, the American diplomat who fashioned the Dayton Peace Accords for Bosnia in 1996, would be an example of one of the power elites. Diplomats like Madeleine Albright and eminent persons like former president Jimmy Carter operate or have operated in this rarified air of power. Unlike the grassroots that, relatively speaking, have little or no power to bring an issue to conclusion, the elite at the top of the pyramid can marshal great resources to make a difference.

Increasingly, however, the most strategic group in the pyramid is the NGO, occupying the middle between the power elites and the grass-roots. For the effective NGO, power is based on relationships. In many ways, this part of the triangle is the most strategic, the most creative, the most entrepreneurial and (again a personal bias) the most fun! The good NGO will have access to the top.

Politics being what they are, NGOs can exercise a great deal of lever-age with political figures. World Vision, for example, has somewhere be-tween one and two million donors in a given year. In a five-year period, there may be as many as five million people out there who have sup-ported the work of this specific international NGO. Five million donors, five million votes! During my tenure, there was a crucial vote in Con-gress on whether or not to provide funds to the United Nations for pre-natal and maternal care in the developing world. A number of Congress members called me for an opinion. On this particular vote, as Congress came into the House chambers, a congressional staff person stood at the door, reminding each member of the position World Vision had taken. On this bill Congress voted for the position that we had espoused.

But the NGO place and space on this triangle is more than simply a question of strategic politics. Nongovernmental organizations also provide critical information to the elite at the top. International NGOs have people on the ground, working at the grassroots, who understand the pain and suffering that is being endured in difficult situations. They see firsthand what is working as well as what is a waste of time and en-ergy. They are remarkably attuned to what a given environment needs for a solution to grab hold, for people to find hope. In short, NGOs have access to information at the grassroots that is needed at the top and, if they are sophisticated at all, an understanding of the conse-quences of what comes down from the top and how those consequences would be played out and implemented at the grassroots.

I mentioned that the power of the NGO in this equation is based on the relationships that are established, both upward and downward. This is critically important in today's world. Given the fact that so many of the conflicts today are resistant to diplomacy, an NGO focused on restoring relationships often bears more promise than one simply based on power politics.

Let me give you a practical example of how all this can work in a positive manner. In the early 1990s, we saw a terrible humanitarian disaster unfold in Somalia, one made much worse by the presence of rival warlords. Along with most of the humanitarian world, World Vision was working in Somalia, desperately trying to save the 75 percent of children under the age of five who were in real danger of starving to death. The lethal combination of famine and internal conflict created a mounting toll of deaths as the fighting intensified, so much so that ultimately the United States sent its own military to Somalia.

The initial landing zone was the city of Mogadishu. This was unfortunate for us, because we were located in Baidoa, 150 miles to the northwest. When the U.S. military landed en masse at Mogadishu, the "bad guys" ran for cover, many of them to Baidoa.

What to do? In the intervening days before the military would make its way to Baidoa, we needed to do something to protect our staff and continue the humanitarian aid that was so desperately needed in that part of the country. In the course of this awkward vulnerability, I spent most of a Saturday on the phone with the Joint Chiefs of Staff, working on a plan to protect the aid workers in Baidoa until our military made an on-the-ground appearance there. The plan was simple: two or three times every day, the Navy would launch F-14 Tomcats from their carriers to fly at supersonic speed low over Baidoa. This can be a terrifying experience for those on the ground. And the mission was eminently successful. The "bad guys" remained totally out of sight. We had no problems from what could have been a most hostile faction disrupting our aid efforts. The work continued, even if the chickens in that area did not lay eggs for weeks.

This very practical solution happened because there was a credible NGO working in Somalia well aware of the situation on the ground and of the consequences of decisions made by people at the highest reaches of power. The credibility of that NGO was such that the power elites became privy to important information through the NGO community and ultimately pursued a course that protected the relatively powerless communities at the grassroots.

Here's another example of the role an NGO can play in bringing solutions to difficult problems. For the past decade, North Korea has been dealing with a massive famine. It may well be that more than 10 percent of the population of 23 million has already succumbed to this famine. The deaths, certainly in excess of two million, have largely been of the very young and the very old.

North Korea needs food. But North Korea has also become one of the political pariahs of our time. Here we have a closed system, an authoritarian ruler who gives all the appearance of caring little for the neediest of his nation, plus a national drive to obtain nuclear weapons and a mindset that suggests they will be used somewhere, sometime, in that part of the world. Suffice it to say, there is very little love lost between the United States and North Korea. Our common history is characterized by war and our common present by vitriolic rhetoric not always seen in diplomatic circles.

But the people have been dying the slow death of starvation. President Ronald Reagan once said, "A starving child knows no politics." Would our government act, however, to aid the starving in a country where the rulers gave all the impression of actively hating the United

States? Politically there was simply no will to help. Neither political party was making the case. None of the polling data placed North Korea high on anyone's radarscope. Our national interest, at least as defined by the people at the top of the pyramid, was not being threatened. Humanitarian food supplies were scarce throughout the world. For all these reasons, perhaps North Korea should be bypassed.

But the NGO community would not let the cries of starving children go unheard. A loose coalition was put together in Washington, D.C., led by World Vision's vice president, Andrew Natsios (currently the administrator for USAID). The coalition devised a strategy to raise awareness inside Washington's Beltway. Ads were taken out in local newspapers, highlighting the need to transcend politics while advocating for the voiceless in North Korea. Meetings with governmental agencies allowed the NGO community to make its case. Not all of these meetings were decorous. Indeed one ended in a shouting match, with Natsios taking on much of the established governmental humanitarian infrastructure. In the end, this advocacy work paid off, perseverance was rewarded, and the ethics of the exercise were more than able to overwhelm the politics of timidity. Food was sent en masse to North Korea. A former, present and perhaps future enemy was engaged with a transcendent act of humanitarian kindness—all made possible because of the power inherent in the NGO community.

A word of caution: there are more than thirty-five thousand NGOs in America today. They vary not only in mission, size and funding support; some are simply better than others. The label alone won't determine the quality. Each has to be evaluated on its own merits, but more about that later.

MAKING THE CASE: FAITH-BASED NGOS

There are secular as well as faith-based NGOs today. Given the nature of this long-term, difficult work, and all other things being equal, I would put my money on the faith-based NGO.

First, motivation is a critically important element in NGO work. For the Christian, that motivation begins with the fact that each of us has been created in the image of God. This is why we care for people we have never met. This is why the starving North Korean is so important to us. Global engagement is involvement in the world that "God so loved." It is more than an ideological issue, greater than political interests, much more powerful than secular morality. Our motivation transcends ideology, politics and secular ethics. We have a theological basis for what we do. The principles inherent in the parable of the good Samaritan are just as valid today as they were when Christ first felt compelled to tell the story. Caring for the world and its subjects is part of our commitment to our God—a faithfulness and obedience to his call and claim on our lives. That is a powerful motivation!

This is the kind of motivation that has produced so many martyrs of the church. It is why the Mennonites stayed in Vietnam when the war raged on and claimed the lives of many who were committed to that place. It is why the Catholic lay order Sant'Egidio persevered for over a decade to facilitate a peace in Mozambique. This is never a question of enjoyment, of money, of prestige or of credit. For the faith-based NGO, it is the motivation that inspired the work of Mother Teresa: obedience to the heavenly call.

Our faith is ultimately the source of our power. When we execute the task with credibility and impact, it is the source of our relevancy as viewed by other actors similarly involved. Lots of people talk. Relatively few "do." For the Christian, *faith* is an action word that compels and propels us to all of the arenas of our world, no matter how difficult. If you watch a good Christian NGO at work, faith will be palpable and totally woven into the fabric of its work. People of faith are the first to arrive and the last to leave.

Second, the trauma of the world cries out for another kind of intervention, an intervention that is based on the need for hope. Many times this is overlooked, but hope has to be created and hope also has to be sustained. I have seen people die, not because they lacked food or water, but because they had lost all hope. As said earlier, our foremost task as Christians is as hope providers. Paul was clear: "We do not want you . . . to grieve like the rest of men, who have no hope" (1 Thessalonians 4:13). And we bear witness to the hope that lies within us. This is our core competency. This is what Christians do. This is how we should be known if we claim to be following the One called Jesus.

But how does hope really work, especially in those hellholes of our world that are given to so much despair? Very simply, something is provided in the present, something both tangible and positive. That "something" might be the aid worker who has consciously chosen to come and work in an environment where it is 123 degrees in the shade. That "something" will be written on the faces of the women in a community when clean water is found and the scourge of Guinea worm is no longer a reminder of their vulnerability. It was the look that the woman gave Margaret Ann at the Ethiopian feeding station when her supply of grain was replenished and she knew life would go on. An act of grace, positive and tangible, takes place in the present that points toward a better future. This is hope.

The death and resurrection of our Lord Jesus were followed by his words: "I am going there to prepare a place for you. And if I go and prepare a place for you, I will come back and take you to be with me that you also may be where I am" (John 14:2-3). The ultimate signs of hope: the reality inherent in the empty tomb, a sovereign God and a church that will prevail against even the gates of hell! Christians have so much that has been made tangible in the "kingdom that has come" that allows us to look with legitimate and credible hope to the "kingdom of our coming Lord."

Christians know a lot about hope. And we are the dispensers of hope. This is the kind of hope that needs to be present in developmental models for sustainability to be achieved. As we extend our "artificial hands" to meet the needs that are so painfully obvious, the best of the faith-based NGOs are exceedingly attractive to those who would like to holistically engage the world.

PICKING THE BEST

There are a number of other issues that go into the evaluation of an effective NGO. Leadership, of course, is critically important. I would never make a major gift to an organization whose leader I did not know or whose vision I did not share. As I noted before, my generation did a much better job of producing politicians than producing leaders. Quite frankly, there is a dearth of good leadership in the NGO community. Titles alone won't tell you much. This is not to say there are no good leaders, but rather that many fall into that vast horde of the average.

Leadership must not be a lost art. When you evaluate an organization based on leadership, make sure this is a characteristic that catches your attention quickly. Former and present employees can give you a pretty good indication of the strength of leadership. Résumés tell you much too. Look for individuals who have been identified with vibrant organizations in the past or who have turned organizations around. Look especially for those individuals who seem to collect good people around them. Energy, enthusiasm and optimism—all emerge in an organization that is properly led.

If the NGO is international, pay close attention to the makeup of the "field" workforce. Is it populated solely by Westerners? Is there only a token expression of the gifts and experiences of nationals? Or does the organization spend a great deal of time on and have an intentional philosophical focus toward staffing its local operations with indigenous employees? The latter is what you are after. Development projects without indigenous employees will never be sustainable. It is as simple as that.

An indigenous workforce will have command of the language, the culture, the folkways and the mores of a given locale. They are the ones who almost never leave, no matter how difficult a situation becomes. I can remember in Somalia when World Vision had a staff in excess of three hundred employees. Only a handful were individuals from other locations, primarily the West. There were many times during Somalia's dark days of the early 1990s when our foreign staff had to be evacuated. The work never missed a beat, however, because we had close to three hundred Somalis who were there to carry on.

A local workforce is philosophically and pragmatically the right way to go. Indeed I would never invest in an international NGO with either my time or my money if it did not employ an indigenous workforce at the point of implementation. An indigenous staff always demonstrates an organization's maturity and speaks very clearly to the soundness of its operations.

Let me return to sustainable solutions. Sadly this is not the obvious goal of many organizations. Any organization that is not trying to provide solutions that endure is one that should raise our deepest suspicions. Band-Aids simply do not work. Chasing the ambulance, following fads and looking for the emergency-of-the-month will do nothing but elicit scorn from the better NGOs and the hardest-working governments.

It is hard to raise the consciousness of a resource-rich nation toward a country experiencing multiple disasters when the donor nation thinks the problem has already been "fixed." Look at the money that has been spent on the continent of Africa in the last thirty years. Relative to the huge amounts invested, there is precious little sustainable development evident today. This takes nothing away from the wonderful examples that go against such a trend (and there are many!), but it still should be an issue of great concern. Donor fatigue will happen and might even be irreparable when there is a long history of Band-Aids applied without solutions that endure. Good organizations know this and plan and work accordingly. Even during relief efforts, when the only thing you can do is triage, good organizations will still sow the seeds for long-term sustainable development.

It is also good to look at an organization's funding base. Where does it get its money? Does it come largely from individuals or does it come from the United States government? Is it cash, or are there high levels of gifts in kind in the income figures? Regardless of how money comes, organizations will understandably try to enhance their revenue numbers, because ultimately that is how you reduce the percentage allocated to overhead. And overhead rates are watched very closely by all the watchdog agencies that report on charitable organizations.

As you might imagine, cash gifts from private individuals tend to be the most flexible, with the fewest strings attached. Private cash also gives an organization resources to properly match a government grant or to ship gifts in kind in a timely manner. Also, when times are tough and organizational retrenchments are called for, those groups with the highest percentage of private donations will have the best chance of keeping their human resources in place. While there is no standard formula for such security, I would look for an organization whose funding base is 70 percent private gifts.

In addition to the amount of private cash, one should look at the number of donors. A broad donor base allows a great deal more predictability in funding than just a few "sugar daddies." Additionally a relatively large number of small gifts might allow an organization to be more recession proof than a few big ones. An individual's gift to an organization is a statement of affirmation and an endorsement from a third party. The more individuals who endorse what an organization is doing, the stronger that organization undoubtedly is.

Finally, a key characteristic you should always look for in an organization engaging today's world is a sensitivity toward, an ability for and an understanding of the role of reconciliation in providing long-term, sustainable solutions. Indeed reconciliation is the ultimate sustainable solution. As I have noted throughout this book, it is the endgame for both the human rights activist and those who occupy the category of realpolitik. Individuals need to be reconciled to one another. Many times there is the need for reconciliation between individuals and their government, and as Christians we know that ultimately there needs to be a bridge of reconciliation built with our God. Anything short of this will speak to an unfinished task, a job not completely done, a cause not properly addressed. Scott Appleby, in his book *The Ambivalence of the Sacred,* makes the case for religious peacemakers in the conflicted arenas of our world:

> Certain aspects of [the politics of forgiveness] fall naturally within the province of religious actors. A politics of forgiveness requires practical wisdom about the healing of memory and the practices leading to genuine reconciliation. It also requires qualities rarely seen in combination: zeal for justice informed by a willingness to forgive; patience, restraint, and persistence in the face of setbacks (e.g., the violation of ceasefires); and, perhaps most crucial, a vast supply of hope—the kind of virtues aspired to by people of faith and nurtured by religious communities.[4]

Anyone serious about global engagement must have a methodology for ameliorating the conflictive relationships that are encountered. It is hard to do relief when the bullets are flying. It is impossible to distribute food when caught in the crossfires of conflict. The good NGO will understand the benefits of mediation, the necessity of conflict resolution

175

and the long-term hope that becomes legitimate with effective heart change, that is, reconciliation.

Ultimately this is yet another reason for looking to the faith-based NGO. While reconciliation is the heart of our gospel, it is also a spirituality. Unfortunately that spirituality is not always evident. But look for it. You will find it in the very best organizations.

No one should be wasting time in the context of our world's present problems. There should be a sense of urgency behind our involvement in and effective engagement of solutions. Identify with an organization for which you need not apologize. Good organizations certainly do exist, and they are one of the most effective ways to extend our "artificial hands" to meet today's needs.

A REGISTER OF EXCELLENCE

I would like to mention some organizations and denominations in which an individual might invest his or her energies. The risk, of course, is that I will be leaving out many more than I include. What I am attempting to do in the following paragraphs is provide an illustrative set of examples of the organizations and institutions that have built good reputations in difficult places. The list is simply that—illustrative—and certainly not exhaustive. (For contact information on these and other good organizations, see appendix two.)

Denominations. Here the history is very clear. The Presbyterians did a wonderful work in China in the nineteenth and early twentieth centuries. The American Baptists get extremely high marks for their work in Burma. In both of these countries, seeds were planted that continue to bear fruit, even in the most difficult circumstances. I have already mentioned my positive bias toward the Mennonites; I have run into people from this denomination in every corner of the globe. Their efforts are always marked by perseverance, persistence, humility and trust—the characteristics that endear them to people who know they are there to help. The work of the Mennonites in Southeast Asia is especially notable.

Speaking of Southeast Asia, we also find there the strong and effective historical roots of the Christian and Missionary Alliance (C&MA). The affection one finds for the C&MA in places like Laos and Vietnam is both palpable and well deserved.

I have also been very impressed by the work of the Adventists. Especially in the area of international religious freedom, they are well organized, wonderfully focused and extremely effective in keeping the flame of religious liberty alive in the cruel corners of our world.

One of the reasons denominations can be so effective is that they have spent intentional time reflecting on proper methodology and then holding their international projects accountable to the best of that reflection. Accountability is not always found in the independent church. Indeed (and I apologize for the generalization of this statement), one should be a little more cautious when assessing the work of independent churches. Accountability is often missing. Historical reflection is not always there. The reluctance of such churches to network with others sometimes robs them of "best practices," a collective body of knowledge that has proven to work well over time.

Human rights. There are extensive human rights NGOs that also work internationally. Once again, caution needs to be exercised regarding the methodologies at play. For example, beware the human rights activist who has nothing to lose. Many of these organizations do not have staff in the field, are not operational at the grassroots and live out their advocacy role in Western countries like the United States. Obviously there is nothing wrong with advocacy, and the voiceless need all the help they can get, but sometimes such groups don't have a realistic understanding of what takes place at points of implementation. It is not enough to raise the level of rhetoric, to engage in high-level finger-pointing, to manipulate guilt to the point of response. One also needs a plan of implementation. How do we respond in a way that will positively change a problem into a solution that endures? It is one thing to speak truth to power, but the really good human rights organizations know something about implementation in the field once that power has been put into motion. If you are interested in a human rights NGO, look for one that consciously tries to bring principles and pragmatics into the same program.

Relief and development. In terms of relief and development agencies, the ones that have been most visible around the world are those that also have had a long history of effective work. In short, they have earned the right to be heard and have certainly earned the right to be affirmed. It will come as no surprise that I am high on World Vision, an organization that has earned its stripes at the community level. World Relief does wonderful work with the church internationally. World Concern also deserves mention, especially for its work throughout Asia.

I am also partial to Mercy Corps, because of its thoughtful theological reflection, which undergirds some very talented people and developmentally sound programs. Similarly, do not forget the Salvation Army. No organization that I am aware of takes a dollar further than they. Their motivation is pure, their perseverance predictable and their humility most endearing. And do not forget the Catholic lay order of Sant'Egidio. This group of individuals employs common sense, godly motivation and what Eugene Peterson captured in the title of one of his books: a long obedience in the same direction. They have persevered in difficult places. Their successes, such as their work in Mozambique, have been most dramatic.

Justice for the poor. Of course, not all faith-based organizations working internationally do so on the basis of relief and development. International Justice Mission (IJM), for example, has focused attention on those who suffer because of the failure to protect the most basic rights of the poor. They serve the millions who suffer under forced prostitution, bonded slavery, illegal detention, torture, illegal land seizures, sexual violence, police and soldier abuse, and other base brutalities that are so frequently at the root of so much hunger, disease, homelessness, illiteracy and human destitution in our world.

The international human rights community has worked with great success over the past fifty years in establishing international norms that condemn such practices, but the new millennium presents a very different challenge, namely how to deliver the promised protections of the law to the vulnerable parts of that world. This is what IJM does better than anyone. They have employed a unique model of individual casework that walks alongside local authorities and community leaders in thousands of cases in the developing world. Specifically IJM has brought to bear the neglected tools of professional criminal investigation, basic legal advocacy and creative applications of international pressure from the U.S. government and other entities. If you are interested in getting involved with an organization that works directly with the implementation of justice, you can do no better than IJM.

Domestic ministries. Not surprisingly, the best organizations are now identified by the people who have run them faithfully for a long time. Individuals who have labored in the domestic vineyards for many years are people like Ray Bakke of International Urban Associates, a man who has dedicated his entire life to work within the city. I think of Ron Sider, who began Evangelicals for Social Action nearly thirty years ago. Eugene Rivers, of Boston TenPoint Coalition, has achieved a great deal through his straight-talking, common sense methodologies for engaging the inner city. Louis Cortez and Bart Campolo of Mission Year, located in Philadelphia, and Jim Wallis of Sojourners in Washington, D.C., are also names that come to mind because of their persistence, indefatigable energy and constant hope. All of these individuals have organizations that have developed around them.

EXTENDING HANDS ALONG OUR JERICHO ROAD

We live in a time of massive human need. For the Christian, denial is not an option. Ignorance is no excuse. We know there are needs unfulfilled, and hopefully we now know there is something that each of us can do. We want to redeem the moment and make the most of the time that our Lord has allowed us to be on this earth, engaging his world. We want to be as shrewd as a serpent, as well as gentle as a dove (see Matthew 10:16). In the words of the Old Testament proverb, we want to make sure "the horse is made ready for the day of battle," knowing that "victory rests with the LORD" (Proverbs 21:31). To paraphrase Zygmunt Bauman, we need to explore all ways to extend our artificial hands to better match what our artificial eyes have shown us.

The Jericho Road of the twenty-first century is littered with bodies—bruised, hurting, stripped of dignity, hungry, despairing—waiting for our intervention. Passion is not enough. We need to choose carefully how we augment our individual resources to replicate what constitutes our best—theologically, philosophically, developmentally and pragmatically. Choose your organization wisely. Your neighbors are counting on you!

IO

HOPE
Can You Describe This?

But in truth it is hard to speak of policy when all that fills the mind is tragedy. The ashes of Manhattan cover the entire land. The pictures wound and wound and wound. The planes slam every time for the first time, the buildings fall every time for the first time. Over and over our brothers and our sisters die. These are the records of a defeat, and of a derangement of the universe. Eloquence is stupid. We have been slaughtered. Even if we live in a culture of forgetting, this we must never forget.

EDITORS OF *THE NEW REPUBLIC*
IN AN ARTICLE PUBLISHED SEPTEMBER 13, 2001

One of the ways for Americans to overcome their trauma is to admit that their suffering is neither unique nor exclusive, that they are connected with so many other human beings who have suffered unanticipated and often protracted injury and fury. As long as they can look at themselves in the mirror of our common humanity.

ARIEL DORFMAN, RECALLING SEPTEMBER 11, 1973,
WHEN CHILE LOST ITS DEMOCRACY IN A MILITARY COUP

Nikolai Yezhov was a brutal man. Anna Akhmatova was one of Russia's greatest poets. Their lives intersected at a prison in Leningrad in the early 1950s. Yezhov was Joseph Stalin's minister of the interior, primarily responsible for smashing any and all opposition to Stalin's reign. One did not need to exercise much political dissent to land in one of Stalin's notorious prisons, where the harshness of the conditions, the torture, the brutality and the despair would break the strongest of men. Anna Akhmatova had two men in prison: her husband and her son.

During the incarcerations that became such a huge part of the Stalinist legacy, women would visit the outside wall of the prison, hoping to see and be seen. At the very least, these women had the ability to sustain hope for loved ones unfortunate enough to be inside. At best, they sometimes could bring food and pass it through the guards to a loved one.

Akhmatova wrote about all of this in her poem "Requiem," her personal lament for those years. In the midst of unspeakable horror, the widespread destruction of innocent people and the loss of human dignity, she gives us this interesting vignette:

> In the terrible years of the Yezhov terror I spent seventeen months waiting in line outside the prison in Leningrad. One day somebody in the crowd identified me. Standing behind me was a woman, with lips blue from the cold, who had, of course, never heard me called by name before. Now she started out of the torpor common to us all and asked me in a whisper (everyone whispered there):
>
> "Can you describe this?"
>
> And I said: "I can."
>
> Then something like a smile passed fleetingly over what had once been her face.[1]

So desperate for an answer to the brokenness and the destruction of her world, the woman reaches out to an individual who carries the dignity and identity of a name. "Can you describe this?"

The bulk of this book has been devoted to becoming acquainted with our changing world. Truth be told, prior to 9/11 it was relatively easy to look at this world with at least a small measure of detachment. We had the option of staying on the balcony instead of immersing ourselves in the world's messiness down on the dance floor in Vietnam or Somalia or Rwanda or Bosnia. We could involve ourselves in the writing of the new rules for global engagement from the safe distance of one of the largest and most economically powerful countries in the world. We could discuss the problems of connecting with humanity at points of suffering, offering the humble apology that suffering was simply not our most familiar exercise. But when mass-scale terror came to our national doorstep on that awful September morning, our lives were forever changed.

"Can you describe this?"

If the beginning of wisdom is calling something by its proper name, the beginning of hope is articulating something in today's reality that gives rise to credible expectations for the future. Secretary of State Colin Powell recently assured us that not only have we experienced the end of the Cold War but also the end of the post-Cold War transition. Clearly the next few years will determine the direction and context of a new strategic era. As such, these are years not unlike those between 1945 and 1950. In that post-war period we saw the Marshall Plan take shape, the creation of the World Bank and the National Security Act of 1947. Nongovernmental organizations like World Vision, CARE and many others had their beginnings during this critical period after years of trauma. The times were rich and full of amazing opportunities, which have since been realized.

If Powell is right, and I think he is, we are (or should be) right now working through the impact and the import of the next fifty years. It is terribly important to understand the launching pad, and the events that created it, for this next strategic era; the unnamed masses of post-September 11 people hunger for an answer. "Can you describe this?"

A New Era

We have discussed previously the focusing role of a common enemy. Indeed we made it through the Cold War because we had such an enemy. The "evil empire" became a rallying cry and allowed us to define ourselves by what we were against. The downside of such an exercise is that we began to lose the ability to articulate what we were really for.

The transitional period since the end of the Cold War has been difficult. We lost that common enemy. It is now time to re-self-define. And I am convinced that this fuzzy, uncertain period of sloppy, tentative half steps can be traced to a poorly defined national identity. The world is desperate for an answer. We must try.

Four Observations

As we begin this new strategic era, I would make four observations, suggest three enhanced expectations (or "silver linings") and leave the reader with two memorable moments that speak to our true identity and ultimate relevance.

An age of paradox. Learning to live in an age of paradox might be the ultimate test of our intellectual credibility. As F. Scott Fitzgerald reminds us, "The test of a first-rate intelligence is the ability to hold two opposed ideas in the mind at the same time, and still retain the ability to function."

As John Paul Lederach has persuasively argued, immediately after the events of September 11 we were forced to grapple with creative tension between different ideas. Consider our impulse to seek "justice": we must face the tension between retributive justice today (that is, accountability) and long-term systemic preventions. Lederach also looks at the question of our real enemy: on the one hand there is the threat from an individual, on the other, the threat from a social milieu. According to him, engagement toward societal change must take place from outside a given country, even while sustainable transformation necessarily comes from within.[2] In each of these issues, two different paths have to be followed simultaneously. These can, at times, be inconsistent exercises, seemingly contradictory. Nevertheless they take place, for the most part, in parallel. This is a paradox.

Apparent contradictions abound in the Christian walk: justice and mercy, free will and divine sovereignty, forgiveness and consequence, dying to self and experiencing new life, saving life by losing it. On their own these pairs are enough to provide thoughtful reflection and intense discourse for a long time. Throw in the snake and the dove, the lion and the lamb, a king born in a stable and a messiah dying on the cross, and we begin to see that Christians should not be surprised by life's seeming contradictions and paradoxes. This suggests, at the very least, that paradox necessitates discernment. And discernment is a gift of the Spirit. As long as we "see through a glass, darkly" (1 Corinthians 13:12 KJV) we also need to cultivate the gift of discernment, especially in this new strategic era.

Paradox, then, should also direct us toward greater humility. We need to admit that we cannot simplify all complexities. Sometimes truth is pursued with a limited vision. That is why the "times" we live in call us to reflect deeply, to listen intently.

Further, some of our hoped-for solutions are not going to be seen in this present age but fall into an eschatological category. "Someday" we will know even as we are known. But for now, this is certainly an age of paradox. Yet we cannot be paralyzed by it; it is simply the nuance of our times. We need to allow ourselves to be humbled by it and to cultivate discernment in the midst of it. We also need to carefully and intentionally embrace paradox. Unfortunately one of the first casualties of war—perhaps especially a "war on terror"—is nuance. Finally, and most importantly, we need to enjoy the mystery of paradox and the yet-to-be-revealed realities that will flow, in time, from it.

An age of ambiguity. The events of 9/11 were a declaration of war in which each faction appealed to the same God. On the one hand, we know we have "evil." But what do we have on the *other* hand? We are still struggling to describe what is on the other hand, but certainly we feel comfortable in calling it "less than evil." "Allah is great" and "God bless America." For too many, however, "our" God offers his blessings draped exclusively in an American flag (this notwithstanding a bracing irony: most American flags are manufactured in China, where only atheists can be in the ruling elites).

The U.S. government enacted sanctions against countries in the past as a clear moral judgment. But we need those countries today in our worldwide fight against terrorism. So sanctions are removed as a pragmatic reality. Seemingly we understand both actions, even as ambiguity clouds our perspective.

We feel slightly uncomfortable asking for God's blessing on our country as we call the enemy "evil," suggesting, by extension, that we have moral rectitude on our side. Honesty compels us to admit that our patriotism is either buttressed by our spirituality or our spirituality is enhanced by a large dose of patriotism. And, of course, maybe we do have right on our side. But that does not lessen the ambiguity.

The war I fought in had more than its share of ambiguity: we lost more than 58,000 Americans. In the succeeding years, more than 150,000 American veterans of the Vietnam War would kill themselves because the ambiguity brought on by a combination of trauma, guilt and pain can be terribly destructive.[3]

None of this is to say, of course, that there are no elements of moral clarity even in the analysis of an ambiguous war. Take, for instance, the practical political effects of the war's outcome for the Vietnamese people's religious freedom, the *sine qua non* of human rights. As I mentioned previously, I had a chance to go back to Danang, Vietnam, in 1989, where I had been stationed. When I saw the squadron of Soviet-built MiG-21s inhabiting the revetments in front of my old hangar, I knew there could have been no more visually provocative reminder that the United States finished second in that conflict. But if we had won—if that old hangar of mine were instead draped in American flags—it is simply beyond question that religious freedom would have been better honored in that country than it is today. Religious freedom, what Thomas Jefferson referred to as our First Freedom, would have been secured. What we at the Institute for Global Engagement see as the *cornerstone freedom,* the absolutely essential component in the building of a values-based civil society, would have been a reality.

I know a great deal about religious persecution in Vietnam today. I have met with pastors who have been through "reeducation" camps, and I am all too familiar with the crackdown during the winter of 2001 in the Central Highlands. Jailings, beatings and even killings continue to this day. When I think of all the brutality against a people simply because of their desire to worship freely, I have no doubt that an American victory would have led to a better peace. And yet *better* is always a relative term; ambiguity always keeps us from the easy answer. Truth is there, but sometimes it is hidden in the predawn darkness of global and moral complexity. In war, neither the cost-benefit analysis of victory nor the cost-benefit analysis of defeat has a single, definitive bottom line.

An age of messiness. The intractable conflicts that I talked about at the beginning of this book are still there. The Balkans continue to simmer. The protracted conflict in Sudan has entered its third decade. Northern Ireland and the Middle East are still held hostage by extremists on all sides.

These are ugly, seemingly endless conflicts. There are times when we can only trust by faith that each one of us has been created in the image of God. Justice has clearly been delayed. Hope is deferred. We continue to remember the sad words of Jeremiah: "The harvest is past, the summer has ended, and we are not saved" (Jeremiah 8:20). Even the incarnation represents the original "dirty business." The Word that became flesh and pitched his tent with us certainly did so with sweat, tears and more than enough dirt under the fingernails. Indeed the sweat poured down at times like great drops of blood. This is the One who continues to dwell among us—and in all the other messy hellholes of our world.

As the old adage goes, a pessimist always has more facts on his or her side. The world's messiness feeds the pessimist's resignation. This is the world where bumper-sticker theology does not quite tell the entire story: the harshness of the journey, the enormous risk of failure, the hopes and fears of all the years. This is the messy world of stable smells and a blood-drenched cross, a world that is as tough on the intellectual neat-freaks as it is on religious people who seemingly have all the answers. With humility, we need to remember that there are times when our airtight theologies, the surety of our "cause" and the political correctness of our religiosity leave us ice-cold. The world is messy, and we have made our contribution!

An age of unanswered questions. Why? Why was America targeted on the eleventh of September? Why did so many innocent people have to die? Why the irreparable void in the hearts of so many loved ones who remain? Why do we have to live in the shadowy world of terrorists and terrorism, where fear pervades and death surprises?

Job asked why: "Why me, Lord?" Certainly this is an understandable question from a righteous man. But God mocks Job in his answer. Indeed it is really an indirect answer, given Job's question. "Where were you when I laid the earth's foundation?" (Job 38:4). And thus begins a divine tirade, a scolding that goes on for a number of chapters. I am sure that by the time God was done, Job was sorry he had even asked the question!

Jeremiah asked why: "Why does the way of the wicked prosper?" (Jeremiah 12:1). This is a great question; like Jeremiah, I would like to know as well. But once again God's answer is indirect: "If you have raced with men on foot and they have worn you out, how can you compete with horses? If you stumble in safe country, how will you manage in the thickets by the Jordan?" (12:5). How strange and challenging this answer must have seemed to Jeremiah. It amounted to this: "It's going to get worse—you ain't seen nothing yet!"

Habakkuk asks a question in the same vein, only more specifically: "Why are you silent while the wicked swallow up those more righteous than themselves?" (Habakkuk 1:13). A great question, deserving of an answer. This question ultimately also is treated to a very strange answer: "The righteous will live by his faith" (2:4).

Even Jesus asked why: "My God, my God, why have you forsaken me?" (Matthew 27:46). And for an answer, there is silence. God says nothing. We are left with the thought that maybe we should not be asking God questions that he has chosen not to answer in the past.

This is all very difficult, but there is no point in entertaining illusions about the suffering of this world or the spiritual challenges this presents. We have just entered a new strategic era! But God's vantage is his own. What he is saying, I think, is this: "Welcome to my world; a world of paradox, ambiguity, messiness and unanswered questions."

Silver Linings

But our responsibilities certainly have not been diminished. In fact, for the Christian, they are as clear today as ever before. We are called to bear witness to the hope that lies within us. This is, indeed, our core competency and the chief characteristic of anyone who claims to follow Jesus. And so we choose optimism for the sake of others, to be hopeful to others, even if at times it is against our better judgment. We look to the silver linings in this mammoth cloud of a post-9/11 experience.

"Can you describe this?" The size of the audience has increased, and many await our answer. I would suggest three helpful outcomes, three silver linings that have emerged from this tragic event.

A new understanding of the "globalization" of suffering. I remember watching, along with a suffering nation, the images of applied evil. Anger, tears and overwhelming sadness turned the day into one of those unique, historic moments when we knew that life was about to change profoundly.

Sometime in the course of that fateful morning, I found myself flashing back to another traumatic time and another difficult experience. I was in Vietnam when the enemy was literally "at the gates." It was the Tet Offensive, and it took us by surprise. We all had felt so powerful, and the war seemed to be turning our way. But now North Vietnamese soldiers were walking the streets of Danang; bullets were zinging through the metal roofs of our "hootches"; pitched battles were taking place at the gates of the American Embassy in Saigon. There were half a million Americans in Vietnam, and we all seemed to be hunkered down in defensive positions trying to figure out this new reality in our lives.

As the North Vietnamese massed for this offensive, their troop concentrations became vulnerable to B-52 raids on their positions. Tet would prove to be a military disaster for the North. But psychologically, the surprise, precision and breadth of the onslaught sowed the seeds of doubt concerning a final victory on our part. Ultimately our will softened, and we left early.

We left early, quite simply, because we could. Vietnam is a long way from America's shores. We decided it was also a long way from our national interest. Two decades later, eighteen American soldiers would be lost in Somalia. We would leave that country early as well—again, because we could. The experience in Somalia would make us a late entry into the genocide of Rwanda, a reluctant participant in the Balkans and a tentative player in Sudan. We seemed to be engaged in an exercise to keep pain and suffering beyond our nation's reach. September 11, 2001, shattered that understandable but unrealistic goal.

There is a passage in Czeslaw Milosz's Nobel Prize-winning autobiography, *Native Realm,* in which the author is watching the skyline of Warsaw literally disappear under the bombardments that accompanied the Polish uprising against the Germans in 1944. "Warsaw I outlawed from my thoughts: a large piece of plain had simply slid into a chasm, burying people and buildings."[4] Years later, in the United States, he laments that Americans have developed "souls of shiny plastic," a suggestion of our inability to conceive the depth of suffering that had taken place during World War II in countries like Poland and Russia. He hauntingly recalls his first arrival into the New York City harbor years earlier: "The gigantic city itself was an outrage because it stood there as if nothing had happened—it had not received a single notch from a bomb—and the people in the streets of Manhattan were free from what flowed in me like molten lead."[5]

Perhaps that was true. It is true no longer. September 11 broke our hearts. Realism will be part of the bond of healing. And a new sense of commonality exists as well. We have seen the application of evil up close, and we cannot remove ourselves from it. We have watched a portion of our skyline disappear, and the suffering of the past century has finally reached our shores. We will never be the same; and therein lies our hope.

The start of a new strategic era. It is amazing how quickly things have changed, for our nation as well as our world. One day we seem to be adopting the stance of a unilateralist. The next we are knee-deep in international coalition building. One day we are accused of isolationism. The next we are feverishly pursuing global engagement.

I have mentioned "force protection" before, using the example of Kosovo. Remember that in the Kosovo conflict, which was fought based on a moral imperative, we still did not allow our planes to descend below fifteen thousand feet to drop their bombs. Essentially we made the statement that no amount of carnage on the ground was worth one American life. Contrast that with the decision that was made on the morning of September 11. If an American airliner full of American citizens was flying toward a populated area with its transponder in the wrong position, we were prepared to shoot it down.

The events of that morning launched the first new war of the twenty-first century. Interestingly the initial weapons of war were not guns or bombs but box cutters, scissors and a blinding rage. We, in turn, responded with our first line of defense, a defense that initially featured not the Marine Corps but the firefighter, the police officer and the postal worker. How quickly things change.

For Christians, there also has to be change. We need to return to a concept suggested by Karl Barth. Speaking metaphorically, Barth challenged the Christian to go forth with a Bible in one hand and a newspaper in the other. How do Christians, viewing life through the lens of the moral imperative—that is, biblical truth—come together with the hard-nosed, security-conscious realists? It is an important question. Now, more than ever, the ability to answer it depends on whether we are sure about our identity as Christians. And our answer will ultimately determine our relevance for this age.

Let me describe the exercise for the Institute for Global Engagement. After the events of September 11, it was immediately clear that security would go to the very top of our hierarchy of values. Any organization that was unable to relate to this issue was going to be irrelevant. The single-issue advocates—that is, those who beat their chests and rise up on their spiritual tiptoes to point out problems without suggesting practical solutions—would take their seat outside the realm of this discussion. The finger-pointers, those who force individuals and governments into corners, the guilt-manipulators and all those who scream righteous indignation, all without a solution in sight, would be dismissed. They would join the ranks of Ahimaaz and all of his followers; they would have nothing to say as the critical powers of the world were engaged.

Because the organizing issue for the Institute for Global Engagement is religious freedom, our relevance was quickly established. There is a very clear nexus point between religious freedom and security. On a pragmatic level, the enemy has declared a religious war. We need to know our enemy; we need to know how he thinks, what motivates him, why he did what he did. Most important, we need to have some idea as to what he might do tomorrow.

The role of religious freedom in the building of a values-based civil society is huge. We can literally track a country on a developmental continuum based on how that country treats religious freedom. As I have suggested elsewhere, when religious freedom is absent, so are most of the other key freedoms, such as speech, association and the press. The absence of these rights stymies a country from developing its people and its structures to be all that they can be, precluding those countries from joining the ranks of the more developed nations of the world. Look at any country where religious freedom is not valued and you will find some form of authoritarianism or despotism, as well as economic or social poverty.

Faith is the one area where we each can make a positive contribution to national and global security. But first we need to know our own faith at its deepest and richest. We need to understand the doctrines of our faith and its eternal verities. We need to know why our faith works and how it functions. We need to assimilate it where we can and to test it in the most difficult areas of our life and world. We need to understand why, in the words of Pascal, "good men believe it to be true."

This would give us a profound position of strength from which to respect the faith of our neighbor. If we understood our faith at its deepest level and enough about our neighbor's in order to show it respect—and if we could somehow find a way for everyone in the world to do the same thing—there would never be sectarian strife. Religious conflict would end. We would develop a greater sensitivity to the things we have in common and, from those points of commonality, a much healthier discussion of the areas that make us legitimately different. We would begin the process of creating "shared meaning," greater understanding and better communication within the human race regarding each other's earnestly held views.

This is where Osama bin Laden got it horribly wrong. He never understood or accepted his own faith in its richness and diversity. Rather he picked and chose those things about his faith that he wanted to practice. It turned out that what he liked most was jihad against the West. This then was not faith, and we really should not even refer to it as religion. Neither is it politics or ideology. What he was left with was a truncated faith, a misunderstood faith and an inappropriately applied faith. In the hands of a zealot, as we now are most painfully aware, such a truncated faith is a very scary thing indeed. Osama bin Laden does not know his own faith, and he certainly has no respect for his neighbor's.

On the eleventh of September, we were attacked by a religious zealot. Our Lebanese friend, Mary, had already demonstrated that people are indeed prepared to die for their faith in this world. Unfortunately there are just as many who are willing to kill for their religion. We cannot and should not attempt to remove this dynamic from an understanding of the new strategic era in which we are engaged.

This rediscovered nexus point between religious freedom and security is what gives us a seat at the table. This makes us relevant. This ensures that we have something to say. Christians cannot ask for more in the world today. The so-called touchy-feely Christians are beginning to make sense to the hard-nosed practitioners of realpolitik. But remember, as British Prime Minister Tony Blair once reminded us, "Our politics only succeed when the realism is as clear as the idealism." Now, more than ever, our theology needs to touch the ground.

An increasing awareness of an interdependent body. Interdependence comes together at points of suffering. As I said before, suffering has never been an area that American Christians have known much about. It's hard for us to connect at this point. Good Friday may have been an international event, but it sometimes seems that the American Christian is only interested in Easter morning. Victory is attractive. Suffering . . . well, suffering is suffering. We need to understand, however, that a holistic view of Scripture does unite the two. Suffering is a part of the Christian package. It is a part of the call and the claim that Christ puts on our lives. Suffering, with all of its ambiguity, messiness and unanswered questions, is still part and parcel of the Christian walk.

An understanding of suffering might even lead us to better comprehend the cost of grace. This is important, because if we do not understand the cost of what has been freely given, our faith will not survive the tough times. Just ask the people of Rwanda. The East African revival of the 1930s had a seemingly deep impact in Rwanda; by 1994 more than 80 percent of that country was Christian. But the faith was soft because the suffering of Christ that enabled grace was never fully known. Today in Rwanda there is nothing cheap about grace! We tend to think of 9/11 as the ultimate assault on contemporary civilization, but during the spring of 1994, Rwanda's citizens were dying at the rate of twelve thousand per day for three solid months. This was the most costly assault on civilization since the Holocaust, and the Rwandan church has yet to recover.

Individual suffering abounds. I vividly remember a visit from an elderly Chinese bishop to my State Department office. He was eighty-two years old at the time and twenty-seven of those years had been spent in jail, most of it in solitary confinement. He told me how the mere moving of his lips in silent prayer would lead to a horrific beating. That is suffering.

I also had a State Department visit from a Vietnamese priest who had spent thirteen years in a "reeducation" camp—again, most of it in solitary confinement. The church suffers! When I begin to understand this more fully, I ask myself, "Where are the marks on the American church?" I have never been beaten. I have never been tortured or jailed. I have never had electrodes hooked up to the sensitive areas of my body. As far as I can remember, in over sixty years I have never even missed a meal.

I was having this kind of discussion a couple of years ago with two Chinese friends. The husband had spent ten years in jail because of his faith. His wife, seated beside him, had spent twenty. I found myself apologizing for a life devoid of suffering. The husband stopped me. "You Christians in the United States have been persecuted," he said. "You have been persecuted by materialism. You have been co-opted by comfort." And then he started quoting Scripture to me (always a convicting experience!). "I know your deeds, that you are neither cold nor hot. I wish you were either one or the other." His voice began to rise: "So, because you are lukewarm—neither hot nor cold—I am about to spit you out of my mouth." (See Revelation 3:15.) Well, no one likes to be lectured to, but when you are across the table from two people who have spent a collective thirty years in jail just because of their faith, you sit in awe and listen.

There is a persecuted church in the world and we need to learn from it. From this interdependent institution, this body that we are told suffers when any one part of it is under duress, we need to learn what the cost of Christianity really is. Gratefully the lessons have become more tangible since September 11.

Two Memorable Moments

The world in which we live today can certainly be sobering. But it is also broadening, challenging and maybe even uniting. We are living in the most exciting time in all of history. This is an adventure, the adventure of a new strategic era for at least the next fifty years—an adventure that has the potential for an enormous final celebration. In that regard, I want to conclude with two stories.

Some time ago, while living in Southern California, Margaret Ann and I decided to join a local Presbyterian church. Let me say at the outset, Presbyterians do not make it easy to become one. (Some have joked that Presbyterians make it more difficult to join the denomination than to go to heaven.) You must go through a program, and there are seven consecutive weeks of classes. There is no denying the value in this approach. There is nothing cheap about being a Presbyterian. One works hard for it, and when you get it, you know you have accomplished something.

I tried to tell the church that their course of instruction was not necessary. They would not hear of it. Even Presbyterian pastors moving to a different community, even those who have been pastors for more than fifty years, would have to take a course in becoming a Presbyterian before they could join a different Presbyterian church. I felt obliged to mention that I had become a Christian during the fifth month of my mother's pregnancy with me. All to no avail. "We have Calvinists that go back a lot further than that!" Everybody takes the course; no exceptions.

And so we submitted ourselves, decently and in order, of course, to the task at hand. Another couple we knew quite well was going through the same program. We agreed that we would follow each lesson of instruction with a meal together at the local Mexican restaurant. At least there would be some fellowship at the end of the day to redeem the time expended on Presbyterianism.

Of course, before we began the instruction, we asked the most important question: "How many lessons can we miss and still graduate on time?" We were pleased to learn that there were two excused absences allowed, a rare moment of grace for a Presbyterian. One night we were coming into the church parking lot in the midst of a wild thunderstorm. There was lightning, thunder, hail and, as only John Calvin could appreciate, a nearby generator was knocked out. The entire block, including the church, turned dark. Class for that night was called off. We now had three excused absences. As we drove out of the parking lot to a premature dinner at the local Mexican restaurant I knew, beyond a shadow of a doubt, that there is a God!

But something happened at one of the sessions that made the entire experience more than worthwhile. We had a woman in our class who was fresh from Iran and new as a Christian. There was a great deal about her faith that was yet to be worked out, a great deal of theology yet to emerge. What she knew for sure was that Jesus loved her. She had been introduced to him recently, was amazed by his unconditional love and loved him back.

One evening the pastor was going through the Apostles' Creed. He was marching through the doctrines of our faith rather quickly—Jesus born of a virgin, suffered under Pontius Pilate . . . was buried . . . arose . . . ascended and is coming back "to judge the quick and the dead." With this last comment—"he's coming back"—the young Iranian woman spoke up from the back of the class: "You mean, he's coming back? I didn't know that!" Her voice was full of awe and gratitude at the same time. "He's coming back!" She had never heard this before.

"He's coming back!" What a beautiful moment. This One whom we all love is returning one day. He's coming back to clean up the mess, to heal the broken world. He's coming back to make sense of the paradoxes, the ambiguities and the messiness of the life in which we find ourselves. He is coming back to answer all those unanswered questions.

The One who loves us unconditionally is coming back. What a tremendous cause for celebration!

John Ortberg, the gifted preacher formerly at Willow Creek Community Church in South Barrington, Illinois, shared this second story at the Leadership Summit in the summer of 2001: A woman was going through some rather severe health problems and felt a need to submit to a battery of tests under the auspices of her doctor. The tests were now complete and the doctor had to share some difficult news. He told the woman she had cancer—a very aggressive form of cancer—and she was not expected to live past the next few months. The doctor counseled her to go and meet with her pastor, to make things ready, to get prepared for the end.

When she went to her pastor, she told him her situation, the premature death that she was anticipating, and more practically, the hymns she wanted sung and the Scriptures she wanted read at the inevitable funeral. After discussing these details with her pastor, she allowed that she had one final request: "At the funeral, I would like to be in an open casket, and I would like to have a fork in my right hand."

Surprised, the pastor encouraged the woman to explain the fork. "It's something that comes from all those potluck dinners we've had here on Wednesday nights," she said. "You know, we have wonderful meals but the highlight of the meal would come when someone came, took our dirty plates, but told us, 'Keep your fork; the best is yet to come.'" The woman went on to tell the pastor that when she heard those words, she knew it was not going to be a Jell-O dessert. No, this was going to be something hefty, perhaps even deep-dish apple pie.

She continued: "I know that there will be those who will feel sorry for me because I died at a relatively young age. I want my service to speak to them. I want it to be a time of celebration. I want to bear witness to the hope that lies within me. Bury me with a fork in my hand. The best is yet to come!"

We engage the world, with all its problems and opportunities, with a Christian message of meaning shared with all those who might listen. It is offered to friends and enemies alike. It is the message of reconciliation, of what Christ has already done. It is a message of grace, a grace that overcomes sin, a grace that is always more abundant. It is a promise from a promise-keeping God that mansions in heaven await us. And if he has gone to prepare that place, he will indeed come again. He is coming back! Be sure to save your fork because the best is yet to come!

We live in a difficult world, and it doesn't promise to get any easier. It is now a world of terror and terrorists, of seemingly intractable intranational identity conflicts, ethnic wars and religious violence. However, we go into that world knowing that someday there will be a new heaven and a new earth. There will come a day when swords will be beaten into plowshares. There will come a time when lions and lambs will lie down together, and both will get a good night's sleep. We can therefore go boldly forward because we have been gifted with the theology of the fork. Truly the best is yet to come.

A CONCLUDING THOUGHT

On September 11, 2001, Margaret Ann and I went to lunch at the Eagle's Nest, a small eatery on the campus of Eastern University. During that lunch, one of my students from the semester before came over to our table. Her eyes were as wide as saucers. The trauma of the morning had not begun to sink in, and she seemed to be in the same state of shock in which each of us found ourselves. She looked at me and the words literally tumbled out of her mouth: "Tell me things."

The formation of her thoughts was simple, yet direct. "Tell me things," which is to say, in the words of another woman at another time, "Can you describe this?" She was asking me to make sense out of the world that was new to her, different than before, changed in ways she could not fathom.

"Tell me things." I felt complimented. I also was humbled.

The world is looking for answers. The world looks to us. We have the exhortation of Scripture and the urgency of the times in which we live. Reconciliation not only will be the essential vision, but the compelling and integrating vision of the twenty-first century. That reconciliation is God's supreme gift, his ultimate legacy. He has offered and defined it in the most dramatic way possible: through the life and death of his Son.

And now we are his agents of the same gift. We are obliged to be appropriately engaged in his world. We are ambassadors of a kingdom whose constitutional foundation is reconciliation; we are his ambassadors of hope. As we search for answers that provide this hope, as we provide tangible expressions today of that which will make tomorrow's hopes credible, as we continue to understand our own identity in the light of his identity, as we make sense of a world that God so loved, when asked, "Can you describe this?" we will answer with a resounding, "Yes!"

EPILOGUE

———————— ✠ ————————

The emotions could not be contained. A Bosnian mother was retelling that awful day almost a decade ago when she lost her husband and her only son at Srebrenica. The Serbian army had overrun the city, one of the few "safe cities" so designated by the United Nations. Irony, impotency and horrific tragedy all came together that day when thousands of Muslim men were rounded up, taken outside the city and summarily executed. The Serbs attempted to hide their genocidal activity and hastily dug mass graves. The memories of loved ones lost, however, continue to keep the world focused on that day when hell let the dogs of war slip on earth.

The mother began to cry as she recounted the final separation from her son. "He was only eighteen. He had such beautiful eyes. They were about to take him away. He looked at me and began to cry. Large tears flowing from those beautiful eyes. I will never forget his face."

The grief continues; this mother realizes that there is absolutely no hope that her son could possibly be alive. He is gone, taken from her, and her life has been devastated by the loss. Mass graves are still being discovered and unearthed, however, and a DNA database has been established. Perhaps his remains could be found and a proper burial provided—a place to visit, to remember a loved one anew, to continue the unbroken process of grief. It is her only hope, the one expectation she has left.

The interview reminded me again how unsolvable today's global problems seem, at least by mortal human standards. War crimes tribunals, the assassination of high-ranking government officials, ethnic apartheid, the presence of foreign troops, criminals unaccounted for—all continue to be part of the present reality in Bosnia and elsewhere. And not only that. Our struggle to contend with the aftermath of 9/11 continues, and our "war on terrorism" (which should be reframed as a war on terror*ists*) threatens to go on for decades. We have fought the Taliban in Afghanistan and Saddam Hussein in Iraq. We fret over North Korea. We are frustrated by the Middle East. We are challenged by the complexities of Indonesia.

Intractability—and the engine that drives this reality, namely our inability to live with our deepest differences—dominates the world stage as never before. Add the explosive growth of AIDS and the dramatic increases in poverty, and we begin to feel overwhelmed by it all. Larger-than-life events drain the emotion from us. In short, there are still plenty of tears to go around.

We live in a world desperately in need of redemption. Individuals, people groups, nations, entire regions of the world need to be reconciled. And the exercise of reconciliation is where our Christian witness is formed. This is where our theology moves us to action. Miroslav Volf's words are succinctly to the point: "What has been done for us must be done by us."

But any call to action must be accompanied by a plan. Throughout this book I have resisted the temptation to make this simply another how-to book. One needs inspiration before perspiration, passion before action. I hope that if this book accomplishes anything, you will be more passionately interested in a world our God continues to love. We are accountable for what we know, however, and responsible for that knowledge being put to good use in those places and instances where we can make a difference. In that vein, I leave you with three to-dos.

Understand your own faith and others'. Get to know your faith at its deepest and richest best, and learn enough about your neighbor's in order to show it respect. This is the ongoing mantra for the Institute for Global Engagement. It is also the single greatest contribution that we can make to homeland security. Sectarian conflicts would cease immediately if we could implement this understanding on a global basis.

We need to know our own faith better. Our faith has to work in difficult circumstances, in difficult places, and yes, especially on the cruel edges of the world. We need to understand its tradition, its doctrines, the eternal truths, the heroes of the faith and how that faith is assimilated individually and applied in community. A superficial faith hurts us, destroys our witness and doesn't hold up in the difficult circumstances of life. We have no option here. For the Christian to be effectively engaged and to confront some of the most difficult problems of a world seemingly out of control, grounding in faith is imperative. Can we have doubts? Sure. A strong faith allows for doubts, knowing we can always return to that profound position of strength that comes from the core of our beliefs, that is, Jesus Christ.

But it is no longer enough to be personally grounded. We need to understand and respect the faiths of others. After the events of 9/11, it was disheartening to see how little we collectively knew of the Islamic faith. Handicapped by a dearth of knowledge and understanding, we developed categories and stereotypes. In some cases, we then went on to demonize the stereotypes we had created. Violence and wars have been started with less. We needed to respect Islam, but we were drifting much closer to hatred.

I am advocating a respect for differences, not their elimination. This is not universalism, or even "easy ecumenism," but rather a celebration of one God in whose image each of us has been crafted. What does respect look like? There was a brief but highly instructive encounter when the U.S. Army went into the holy city of Najaf midway through the Iraq War. A rumor began to circulate within the city that the Army was marching into the sacred mosque. An angry, unpredictable crowd quickly gathered and confronted the American soldiers. The potential for a disastrous confrontation was real. The colonel in charge was ready. He instructed his soldiers: "Look them in the eye. Smile. Take a step backwards. Kneel. Hold your weapon out in front of you, upside down."

The tension immediately dropped. The Iraqis saw a different reality than what had been rumored. They were being respected, and it is hard to be angry with people who are demonstrating that respect.

Know your faith. Respect your neighbor's. This is the antidote to the Osama bin Ladens of the world. This is also what Jesus would have done!

Be better educated about our world. America wields awesome international power today. It is incumbent on American citizens to know more about the world in which this power is unleashed. Ignorance has never been an excuse and it certainly isn't one now. The information is there; knowledge has exploded and the technology to gather and analyze that knowledge has kept up. Books, periodicals, newspapers, websites, seminars and even television have collectively reproduced the kind of global information that should inform our lives.

Discernment, wisdom and an open mind will be necessary accoutrements for effectively assimilating knowledge. Not all scholars have something to say; not all books are worth the paper they are printed on. But good source material always rises to the top. Solid scholarship bests stunning rhetoric. Good analysis eliminates preconceived bias. Carefully done, the pursuit of global information can put nuance into our conclusions and sophistication into our implementation. With the exception of classified materials, all of us have at our disposal the information necessary to properly understand the global issues of our day. This is a gift that cannot be ignored.

Employ a methodology that enhances the message. For the Christian, the methodology for the message is reconciliation. Like never before, this timeless message needs to be seen by a hurting, fragile and disbelieving world. The strength of the message is always in its incarnation—the Word becoming flesh. What the world needs most is something we have individually experienced. "What has been done for us must be done by us."

The heart of this book has stressed the elements of this methodology: truth, mercy, grace, justice and peace. The best ways to give these elements away is to faithfully demonstrate them in every day of our lives. Very simply, our lives should provoke the questions for which Christ's message of reconciliation is the answer.

Reconciliation works in every corner of the world, with all peoples of the world. It overcomes corporate evil and personal sin. It enhances the best of our humanity while treating our worst with both mercy and justice. A reconciled world is a redeemed world, filling the void of our individual hearts and the empty space of failed ideologies and institutions. Reconciliation can turn nations back to God as well as make God-fearing societies more attractive to the rest of the world. Is it any wonder that it has been called "good news"?

A devout Christian who is knowledgeable of the world she or he inhabits and who humbly and respectfully implements the core message of the gospel is a major tool in righting the course of a world adrift. This is not the time to "hide the light under a bushel." Indeed the world has been *forced* to confront the reality of religion and faith as major components in making sense of the world in which we live. Geopolitics is not complete without a thorough analysis of the role of religion. A call to action from a world desperate for answers is now being issued through secular lips.

We have an amazing opportunity for the world to see a faith in action, a faith that *works*. That world can come to experience the very presence of a sovereign God, in whom no issues are intractable. That world can be exposed to the ultimate redemption strategy of an only son sacrificially committed to all the peoples of the world. Once for all, and for all time—the ultimate expression of relevance.

The need has never been greater, the timing never more clear, the message never more appropriate. We still live in a world of tears. But Jesus understands; he cried over Jerusalem, and I suspect he cried again when that only son of a Bosnian mother was led away to his death. Jesus certainly understands the power struggle between good and evil. He knows all there is to know about a life prematurely ended. And God the Father, who hid his own tears in the darkness of Calvary, also knows the pain of losing an only child.

But that child will return! The resurrected Jesus will return to create a new heaven and a new earth, where there will be no more tears. Until that glorious day, we work—wisely, humbly, justly—as ambassadors of hope.

APPENDIX 1

The Institute for Global Engagement's
Principles of Engagement

KNOW HIM

Know your maker—seek to understand his heart and make his passions yours. Know your faith at its deepest and richest best, and enough about your neighbor's faith to respect it.

Sense God's timing. Practice patience. Be brave enough to engage without excuse, strong enough to refuse recklessness.

KNOW YOURSELF

Understand your strengths—and weaknesses—and how they impact your relationships. Do no harm.

Cultivate the characteristics of the biblical metaphors for global engagement: the streetwise common sense of the *snake,* the gentle humility of the *dove,* the wise statesmanship of the *ambassador.*

Pray for the full armor of God. Be transparent, predictable, accountable and responsible. Make hope tangible in the present. Take no credit. Give away learnings. Act incarnationally and establish the worth of the gospel so that the truth might be revealed.

KNOW HIS WORLD

This is God's world. He is deeply in love with it. We "plant and water"; he brings the increase. We "prepare the horse for battle; but victory rests with the Lord." Let God keep score.

Know history—political and cultural, yours and theirs. Know all of the questions, not just some of the answers. Understand geopolitical complexity and local nuance. But realize that God is already there. Recognize that the adjective *intractable* is an insult to a sovereign Lord.

Pray over the land. Pray for discernment to take place, for wisdom to reveal itself. Pray with intentionality. Pray specifically for key individuals involved.

Find partners. Who has been trustworthy, credible, persevering and relevant? Build relationships that endure. "Whoever is not against us is for us." Remember, the Commandment to love was given before the Commission to go.

Act comprehensively. What is the art of the possible? Put yourself in everybody else's shoes. Develop a policy and a supporting strategy around objectives formed in faith. Continuously reassess both policy and concomitant strategy.

And remember: global engagement has a face. A difference is made, a plan is enacted, a transformation takes place one life at a time . . . a life already made in the image of God.

APPENDIX 2
Faith-Based/International NGOs

Adventist Development & Relief Agency International (ADRA)
Ralph S. Watts, President
12501 Old Columbia Pike
Silver Spring, MD 30905
Phone: 301-680-6366
Fax: 301-680-6370
104100.140@compuserve.com
www.adra.org

American Baptist Churches
588 North Gulph Road
King of Prussia, PA 19406
Phone: 610-768-2000
www.abc-usa.org

Boston TenPoint Coalition (Eugene Rivers)
Mark Scott, Executive Director
National Ten-Point Leadership Foundation
411 Washington Street
Boston, MA 02108-5223
Phone: 617-282-6704
http://bostontenpt.users2.50megs.com/

Carnegie Endowment for International Peace
1779 Massachusetts Avenue NW
Washington, DC 20036-2103
Phone: 202-483-7600
Fax: 202-483-1840
info@ceip.org
www.ceip.org

Catholic Relief Services (CRS)
209 West Fayette Street
Baltimore, MD 21201-3443
Phone: 410-625-2220
Fax: 410-685-1635
webmaster@catholicrelief.org
www.catholicrelief.org

Christian Reformed World Relief Committee (CRWRC)
2850 Kalamazoo Avenue SE
Grand Rapids, MI 43560-0600
Phone: 616-224-0740
Fax: 616-224-0806
dgraffb@crcna.org
www.crwrc.org

Compassion International
3955 Cragwood Drive
PO Box 7000
Colorado Springs, CO 80933
Phone: 719-594-9900
www.compassion.com

Defense Prisoner of War/Missing Personnel Office
2400 Defense Pentagon
Washington, DC 20301-2400
www.dtic.mil/dpmo/

Evangelical Environmental Network (EEN)
10 Lancaster Avenue
Wynnewood, PA 19096-3495
Phone: 610-645-9392
Fax: 610-649-8090
een@creationcare.org
www.creationcare.org

Evangelicals for Social Action
10 E. Lancaster Avenue
Wynnewood, PA 19096-3495
Phone: 610-645-9390
www.esa-online.org

Food for the Hungry
7729 Greenway Road
Scottsdale, AZ 85260
Phone: 480-998-3100
Fax: 480-998-4806
hunger@fh.org
www.fh.org

International Aid
17011 West Hickory
Spring Lake, MI 49456
Phone: 616-846-7490
Fax: 616-846-3842
ia@internationalaid.org
www.internationalaid.org

International Justice Mission (IJM)
PO Box 58147
Washington, DC 20037-8147
Phone: 703-465-5495

Fax: 703-465-5499
contact@ijm.org
www.ijm.org

International Teams: US Urban and Ethnic Ministries
2300 South Millard Avenue
Chicago, IL 60623
Phone: 773-522-9636
www.iteams.org

MAP International
PO Box 58147
Washington, DC 20037-8147
Phone: 912-265-6010 or 800-225-8550
Fax: 912-265-6170
map@map.org
www.map.org

Medical Ambassadors International
PO Box 576645
Modesto, CA 95357-6645
Phone: 209-524-0600
Fax: 209-571-3538
info@med-amb.org
www.medicalambassadors.org

Mennonite Church USA
722 Main St., PO Box 347
Newton, KS 67114-0347
Phone: 316-283-5100
Fax: 316-283-0454
www.mennoniteusa.org

Mercy Corps
Dept. W
3015 SW First
Portland, OR 97201
www.mercycorps.org

Mercy Ships
PO Box 2020
Garden Valley, TX 75771-2020
Phone: 903-882-0887
Fax: 903-882-0336
info@mercyships.org
www.mercyships.org

Mission Aviation Fellowship (MAF)
PO Box 3202
1849 Wabash Avenue
Redlands, CA 92373-0998
Phone: 909-794-1151
Fax: 909-794-3016
Maf-us@maf.org
www.maf.org

Mission Year (Bart Campolo)
990 Buttonwood Street
Philadelphia, PA 19123
Phone: 888-340-YEAR
Fax: 215-763-6204
info@missionyear.org
www.missionyear.org

Northwest Medical Teams International (NWMTI)
PO Box 10
Portland, OR 97207-0010

Phone: 503-624-1000
Fax: 503-624-1001
mail@nwmti.org
www.nwmti.org

Opportunity International
360 W. Butterfield Road, Suite 225
Elmhurst, IL 60126
PO Box 3695
Oak Brook, IL 60522
Phone: 630-279-9300
Fax: 630-279-3107
getinfo@opportunity.org
www.opportunity.org

Presbyterian Church (U.S.A.)
100 Witherspoon Street
Louisville, KY 40202-1396
Phone: 800-872-3283
www.pcusa.org

Salvation Army World Services Office
615 Slaters Lane
PO Box 269
Alexandria, VA 22313
Phone: 703-684-5528
Fax: 703-684-5536
www.salvationarmyusa.org

Samaritan's Purse
PO Box 3000
Route 4, Bamboo Road
Boone, NC 28607
Phone: 704-262-1980

Fax: 704-262-1796
www.samaritanspurse.org

Sant'Egidio, Community of
560 Riverside Drive, Apartment 13P
New York, NY 10027
Phone: 212-663-1483
Fax: 212-663-4178
info@santegidio.org
www.santegidio.org

Sojourners (Jim Wallis)
2401 15th Street NW
Washington, DC 20009
Phone: 202-328-8842 or 800-714-7474
Fax: 202-328-8757
sojourners@sojo.net
www.sojo.net

USAID
Ronald Reagan Building
Washington, DC 20423-1000
Phone: 202-712-4810
Fax: 202-216-3524
www.usaid.gov

United States Commission on International Religious Freedom (USCIRF)
800 N. Capitol Street NW, Suite 790
Washington, DC 20002
Phone: 202-523-3240
Fax: 202-523-5020
communications@uscirf.org
www.uscirf.org

World Concern
19303 Fremont Avenue North
Seattle, WA 98133
Phone: 206-546-7201
Fax: 206-546-7269
www.worldconcern.org

World Relief
7 East Baltimore St.
Baltimore, MD 21202
Phone: 443-451-1900
worldrelief@wr.org
www.wr.org

World Vision
220 I Street NE, Suite 270
Washington, DC 20002
Phone: 202-547-3743
Fax: 202-547-4834
www.worldvision.org

World Vision United States
PO Box 9716
Federal Way, WA 98063-9716
Phone: 888-511-6598

Notes

Chapter 1: Relevance
[1]Philip Gourevitch, *We Wish to Inform You That Tomorrow We Will Be Killed with Our Families: Stories of Rwanda* (New York: Farrar, Straus & Giroux, 1998), p. 267.

Chapter 2: Challenge
[1]The United Nations High Commission for Refugees, "Refugees by Numbers 2003," p. 5.
[2]UNAIDS/UNICEF factsheet, "Children Orphaned by AIDS in Sub-Saharan Africa," 2003.
[3]David Manuel, *Bosnia: Hope in the Ashes* (Brewster, Mass.: Paraclete, 1996), p. 82.
[4]Slavenka Drakulic, *Balkan Express: Fragments from the Other Side of War* (New York: Norton, 1993).

Chapter 3: Diversity
[1]John Paul Lederach, *The Journey Toward Reconciliation* (Scottdale, Penn.: Herald, 1999), pp. 47-48.
[2]Miroslav Volf, *Exclusion and Embrace: A Theological Exploration of Identity, Otherness, and Reconciliation* (Nashville: Abingdon, 1996), p. 91.
[3]Ibid., p. 57.
[4]Ibid., p. 75.

Chapter 5: Mercy
[1]Jürgen Moltmann, as cited in Miroslav Volf, *Exclusion and Embrace* (Nashville: Abingdon, 1996), p. 122.
[2]Antoine Rutayisier, *Faith Under Fire* (Essex, U.K.: Victoria House, 1998), pp. 11-12.

Chapter 7: Justice

[1]Miroslav Volf, *Exclusion and Embrace* (Nashville: Abingdon, 1996), p. 199.
[2]Ibid., pp. 193-97.
[3]Ibid., p. 222.
[4]Ibid., pp. 230-31.

Chapter 8: Peace

[1]Glen Stassen, *Just Peacemaking: Transforming Initiatives for Justice and Peace* (Louisville, Ky.: Westminster John Knox, 1992), p. 108.

Chapter 9: Effectiveness

[1]Zygmunt Bauman, "Whatever Happened to Compassion?" in *The Moral Universe,* ed. Tom Bentley and Daniel Stedman Jones (London: Demos, 2002), p. 2. Full text available at <www.demos.co.uk/catalogue/default.aspx?id=45>.
[2]Ibid.
[3]Jessica Mathews, "Power Shift," *Foreign Affairs* 76-1 (Jan./Feb. 1997): 53.
[4]Scott Appleby, *The Ambivalence of the Sacred* (Lanham, Md.: Rowman & Littlefield, 2000), p. 171.

Chapter 10: Hope

[1]Anna Akhmatova, *Atlantic Monthly,* February 1973, p. 62. A translation by S. Kunitz and M. Hayward of "Instead of Preface," the first titled section of "Requiem."
[2]John Paul Lederach, "Quo Vadia? Reframing Terror from the Perspective of Conflict Resolution," an essay presented at the University of California, Irvine, Townhall Meeting, October 24, 2001, for the Joan B. Kroc Institute <www.nd.edu/~krocinst/sept11/ledquo.html>.
[3]Chuck Dean, *Nam Vet* (Portland: Multnomah, 1990), p. 39.
[4]Czeslaw Milosz, *Native Realm* (New York: Doubleday, 1981), p. 255.
[5]Ibid., p. 265.

About the Institute for Global Engagement

For every thousand hacking at the leaves of evil,
there is one striking at the root.

HENRY DAVID THOREAU

The Institute for Global Engagement (IGE) is a "think tank with legs," created to develop sustainable environments for religious freedom worldwide and to inspire and equip emerging leaders with faith-based methodologies of engagement. Founded by Robert A. Seiple, the first-ever U.S. Ambassador-at-Large for International Religious Freedom, IGE uniquely combines strategic analysis with an operational component that seeks solutions to complex political and religious problems in difficult parts of the world.

In this age of widespread religious conflict, pluralism and change, finding such solutions requires a deep understanding of geopolitical realities as well as an approach that is "as shrewd as snakes and innocent as doves" (Matthew 10:16). To meet this challenge, IGE partners with governments, religious organizations, scholars, practitioners and international advocacy groups to take on innovative projects that strike at the root of religious intolerance and educate emerging leaders to take religion seriously in their consideration of international affairs.

Working simultaneously at government and grassroots levels, IGE seeks to create a level playing field for people of all faiths, including those who choose not to believe. (That true faith must be freely chosen is, from our Christian perspective, a foundational belief.) This top-down and bottom-up strategy is based on carefully cultivated relationships. It is the kind of quiet diplomacy that will never be on television or even on our website, but it goes on—day by day, one life at a time for a lifetime—in a manner that is congruent with the diverse cultures in which we work. We take this approach because those who suffer persecution need to know that we have not forgotten their faith, or ours.

A history of religious persecution will show, unfortunately, that Christians sometimes contribute inadvertently to the problem by responding to injustice with a pure motivation but a poor, culturally inappropriate methodology. As a means of addressing this concern, IGE has developed three leadership programs to inspire and equip Christian leaders who have a heart for engaging their world in a more sophisticated way. These programs establish a safe and creative space in which Christians, regardless of their vocation, can practically consider the pressing international issues of the day. It is in this space that a candid intrafaith discussion can take place, the precursor to the interfaith dialogue that our times demand. These programs include Global Engagement Forums held in the United States and abroad; the Council on Faith & International Affairs; and the Master of Arts in Global Engagement.

Nondenominational and nonpartisan, the Institute for Global Engagement works proactively with government and grassroots leaders to advance freedom of belief and practice; equips emerging leaders with a strategic and practical understanding of the world; demands thoughtful and comprehensive analysis as the basis for innovative solutions; provides thought leadership on key issues of faith and politics; and seeks partnership with like-minded organizations of all faiths.

If this kind of work is of interest to you, please visit our website at <www .globalengagement.org>.

The Institute for Global Engagement
PO Box 14477
Washington, DC 20044
Phone: 443-262-9872
Fax: 443-262-9873
www.globalengagement.org